Nancy Wass
O'Dell

CELEBRATION
OF DISCIPLINE

CELEBRATION OF DISCIPLINE

The Path to Spiritual Growth

Richard J. Foster

1817

Published in San Francisco by

HARPER & ROW, PUBLISHERS

New York, Hagerstown, San Francisco, London

Designed by Janice Stern

Library of Congress Cataloging in Publication Data

Foster, Richard J.
   THE CELEBRATION OF DISCIPLINE.

   1. Spiritual life—Society of Friends authors.
I. Title.
BV4501.2.F655   1978   248'.48'96   77-20444
ISBN 0-06-062831-6

---

   80 81 82 10 9 8

To Carolynn

wife, counselor, companion, encourager

CONTENTS

FOREWORD

There are many books concerned with the inner life, but there are not many that combine real originality with intellectual integrity. Yet it is exactly this combination which Richard Foster has been able to produce. Steeped as he is in the devotional classics, the author has given us a careful study that may, itself, be valued for a long time. Though the present volume demonstrates indebtedness to the Classics, it is not a book about them; it represents, instead, genuinely original work.

What strikes us at once is the comprehensive character of the current undertaking. Many contemporary books deal with particular aspects of the inner life, but this one is different in that it deals with an astonishing variety of important topics, much of its freshness of treatment arising from its boldness. The author has undertaken to examine a wide spectrum of experience, from confession to simplicity to joy. Since the finished product is the outcome of wide reading and careful thinking, it is not the sort of book that can be dashed off quickly or cheaply.

The sources of insight are varied, the chief ones being the Holy Scriptures, and the recognized classics of devotion, but these are not the only fountains from which the author draws. The careful reader soon recognizes a large indebtedness to secular thinkers as well. In view of the fact that the author is himself a Quaker, it is not surprising that the contributions of the classic Quaker writers are prominent. These include the works of George Fox, John Woolman, Hannah Whitall Smith, Thomas Kelly and many more. The purpose here is not sectarian but genuinely ecumenical, since important insights ought never to be limited to the group from which they arise. What we are given, accordingly, is an example of the catholicity of sharing.

The treatment of simplicity is especially valuable, partly because it is not simple. Indeed the ten "controlling principles" concerning simplicity, which are explained in Chapter VI, are themselves sufficient justification for the appearance of another book on the spiritual life. The ten principles enunciated, while rooted in ancient wisdom, are made astonishingly contemporary.

The author understands very well that the emphasis upon simplicity may itself become a snare. This is why he will not settle for anything so obvious as the adoption of a plain garb, though he can say tersely, "Hang the fashions. Buy only what you need." Here is a radical proposal which, if widely adopted, would be immensely liberating to people who are the victims of the advertisers, particularly those on television. A genuine cultural revolution would ensue if considerable numbers were to obey the trenchant command, "De-accumulate."

The greatest problems of our time are not technological, for these we handle fairly well. They are not even political or economic, because the difficulties in these areas, glaring as they may be, are largely derivative. The greatest problems are moral and spiritual, and unless we can make some progress in these realms, we may not even survive. This is how advanced cultures have declined in the past. It is for this reason that I welcome a really mature work on the cultivation of the life of the spirit.

D. Elton Trueblood

ACKNOWLEDGMENTS

Books are best written in community. I am deeply indebted to those whose lives have surrounded mine and have given substance to the ideas in this book. It was through the friendship and teaching of Dallas Willard that I first saw the meaning and necessity of the Spiritual Disciplines. For four years and more he was my mentor in the Disciplines. His life is the embodiment of the principles in this book.

I owe much to Bess Bulgin, who carefully and prayerfully read each line of this book many times over. Her feel for rhythm has greatly enhanced its readability. Ken and Doris Boyce helped me more than they will ever know by their constant encouragement and enthusiasm. Connie Varce is the finest administrative secretary anywhere and her help in typing, grammar and optimism added a great deal. Mary Myton worked endlessly in typing both rough draft and the final manuscript. Stan Thornburg taught me about the Discipline of Service with his words and his life. Rachel Hinshaw graciously offered her skills as a professional proofreader. My special thanks to Newberg Friends Church for releasing me to have time to write in the final weeks of this book, and especially to Ron Woodward, whose pastoral load of necessity increased as mine decreased.

My children, Joel and Nathan, were incredibly patient in allowing their daddy to cut short games and stories more than once. With the completion of this book comes the joy of once again lengthening those games and stories.

1. THE SPIRITUAL DISCIPLINES: DOOR TO LIBERATION

I go through life as a transient on his way to eternity, made in the image of God but with that image debased, needing to be taught how to meditate, to worship, to think.—Donald Coggan, Archbishop of Canterbury

Superficiality is the curse of our age. The doctrine of instant satisfaction is a primary spiritual problem. The desperate need today is not for a greater number of intelligent people, or gifted people, but for deep people.

The classical Disciplines* of the spiritual life call us to move beyond surface living into the depths. They invite us to explore the inner caverns of the spiritual realm. They urge us to be the answer to a hollow world. John Woolman counseled, "It is good for thee to dwell deep, that thou mayest feel and understand the spirits of people." [1]

We must not be led to believe that the Disciplines are for spiritual giants and hence beyond our reach, or for contemplatives who devote all their time to prayer and meditation. Far from it. God intends the Disciplines of the spiritual life to be for ordinary human beings: people who have jobs, who care for children, who must wash dishes and mow lawns. In fact, the Disciplines are best exercised in the midst of our normal daily activities. If they are to have any transforming effect, the effect must be found in the ordinary junctures of human life: in our relationships with our husband or wife, our brothers and sisters, our friends and neighbors.

---

* You may be wondering why the Disciplines described in this book are termed "classical." They are not classical merely because they are ancient, although they have been practiced by sincere people over the centuries. The Disciplines are classical because they are *central* to experiential Christianity. In one form or another all of the devotional masters have affirmed the necessity of the Disciplines.

Neither should we think of the Spiritual Disciplines as some dull drudgery aimed at exterminating laughter from the face of the earth. Joy is the keynote of all the Disciplines. The purpose of the Disciplines is liberation from the stifling slavery to self-interest and fear. When one's inner spirit is set free from all that holds it down, that can hardly be described as dull drudgery. Singing, dancing, even shouting characterize the Disciplines of the spiritual life.

In one important sense, the Spiritual Disciplines are not hard.* We need not be well advanced in matters of theology to practice the Disciplines. Recent converts—for that matter people who have not yet turned their lives over to Jesus Christ—should practice them. The primary requirement is a longing after God. The psalmist wrote, "As the hart longs for flowing streams, so longs my soul for thee, O God. My soul thirsts for God, for the Living God" (Ps. 42:1, 2).

Beginners are welcome. I, too, am a beginner, even and *especially* after a number of years of practicing every Discipline discussed in this book. As Thomas Merton said, "We do not want to be beginners. But let us be convinced of the fact that we will never be anything else but beginners all our life!" [2]

Psalm 42:7 reads "Deep calls to deep." Perhaps somewhere in the subterranean chambers of your life you have heard the call to deeper, fuller living. Perhaps you have become weary of frothy experiences and shallow teaching. Every now and then you have caught glimpses, hints of something more than you have known. Inwardly you have longed to launch out into the deep.

Those who have heard the distant call deep within and who desire to explore the world of the Spiritual Disciplines are immediately faced with two difficulties. The first is philosophic. The materialistic base of our age has become so pervasive that it has given people grave doubts about their ability to reach beyond the physical world. Many first-rate scientists have passed beyond such doubts, knowing that we cannot be confined to a space-time box. But the average person is influenced by popular science which is a generation behind the times and is prejudiced against the nonmaterial world.

It is hard to overstate how saturated we are with the mentality of popular science. Meditation, for example, if allowed at all, is not thought of as contact with a real spiritual world but as psychological

* In another sense, they are hard indeed—that is a theme we will develop later.

manipulation. Usually people will tolerate a brief dabbling in the "inward journey," but then it is time to get on with *real* business in the *real* world. We need the courage to move beyond the prejudice of our age and affirm with our best scientists that there exists more than the material world. In intellectual honesty, we should be willing to study and explore this other realm with all the rigor and determination we would give to any field of research.

The second difficulty is a practical one. We simply do not know how to go about exploring the inward life. That has not always been true. In the first century and earlier, it was not necessary to give instruction on how to "do" the Disciplines of the spiritual life. The Bible called people to such Disciplines as fasting, meditation, worship and celebration and gave almost no instruction about how to do them. The reason for that is easy to see. Those Disciplines were so frequently practiced and such a part of the general culture that the "how to" was common knowledge. Fasting, for example, was so common that no one had to ask what to eat before a fast, or how to break a fast, or how to avoid dizziness while fasting—everyone already knew.

That is not true of our generation. Today there is an abysmal ignorance of the most simple and practical aspects of nearly all the classic Spiritual Disciplines. Hence any book written on the subject must take that need into account and provide practical instruction on the mechanics of the Disciplines. One word of caution, however, must be given at the outset; to know the mechanics does not mean that we are practicing the Discipline. The Spiritual Disciplines are an inward and spiritual reality and the inner attitude of the heart is far more crucial than the mechanics for coming into the reality of the spiritual life.

The Slavery of Ingrained Habits

We are accustomed to thinking of sin as individual acts of disobedience to God. That is true enough as far as it goes, but Scripture goes much farther.* In Romans the apostle Paul frequently referred to sin as a condition that plagues the human race (i.e., Rom. 3:9–18). Sin as a condition works its way out through the "bodily members"; that is,

---

* Sin is such a complex matter that the Hebrew language has eight different words for it, and all eight are found in the Bible.

the ingrained habits of the body (Rom. 7:5ff.). And there is no slavery that can compare to the slavery of ingrained habits of sin.

In Isaiah 57:20 we are told, "The wicked are like the tossing of the sea; for it cannot rest, and its waters toss up mire and dirt." The sea does not need to do anything special to produce mire and dirt; that is the result of its natural motions. That is also true of us when we are under the condition of sin. The natural motions of our lives produce mire and dirt. Sin is part of the internal structure of our lives. No special effort is needed. No wonder we feel trapped.

Our ordinary method of dealing with ingrained sin is to launch a frontal attack. We rely on our willpower and determination. Whatever the issue for us may be—anger, bitterness, gluttony, pride, sexual lust, alcohol, fear—we determine never to do it again; we pray against it, fight against it, set our will against it. But it is all in vain, and we find ourselves once again morally bankrupt or, worse yet, so proud of our external righteousness that "whitened sepulchers" is a mild description of our condition. Heini Arnold in his excellent little book entitled *Freedom from Sinful Thoughts* writes, "We . . . want to make it quite clear that we cannot free and purify our own heart by exerting our own 'will.' "[3]

In Colossians Paul listed some of the outward forms people use to control sin: "touch not, taste not, handle not." He then added that these things "have indeed a show of wisdom in *will worship*" (Col. 2:20–23, KJV). "Will worship"—what a telling phrase, and how descriptive of so much of our lives! The moment we feel we can succeed and attain victory over our sin by the strength of our will alone is the moment we are worshiping the will. Isn't it ironic that Paul looked at our most strenuous efforts in the spiritual walk and called it idolatry: "will worship"?

Willpower will never succeed in dealing with the deeply ingrained habits of sin. Emmet Fox writes, "As soon as you resist mentally any undesirable or unwanted circumstance, you thereby endow it with more power—power which it will use against you, and you will have depleted your own resources to that exact extent."[4] Heini Arnold concludes, "As long as we think we can save ourselves by our own will power, we will only make the evil in us stronger than ever."[5] This same truth has been experienced by all of the great writers of the devotional life from St. John of the Cross to Evelyn Underhill.

"Will worship" may be able to have an outward show of success for a time, but in the cracks and crevices of our lives, our deep inner condition will always be revealed. Jesus described that condition when He spoke of the outward show of righteousness of the Pharisees. "Out of the abundance of the heart the mouth speaks. . . . I tell you, on the day of judgment men will render account for every *careless word* they utter" (Mt. 12:34–36). By dint of will people can make a good showing for a time, but sooner or later there will come the unguarded moment when the "careless word" will slip out to reveal the true condition of the heart. If we are full of compassion, it will be revealed; if we are full of bitterness, that also will be manifested.

It is not that we intend to be that way. We have no intention of exploding with anger or of parading a sticky arrogance, but when we are with people, what we *are* comes out. Though we may try to hide these things with all our might, we are betrayed by our eyes, our tongue, our chin, our hands, our whole body language. Willpower has no defense against the careless word, the unguarded moment. The will has the same deficiency as the law—it can deal only with externals. It is not sufficient to bring about the necessary transformation of the inner spirit.

The Spiritual Disciplines Open the Door

When we despair of gaining inner transformation through human powers of will and determination, we are open to a wonderful new realization: inner righteousness is a gift from God to be graciously received. The needed change within us is God's work, not ours. The demand is for an inside job, and only God can work from the inside. We cannot attain or earn this righteousness of the kingdom of God; it is a grace that is given.

In the book of Romans the apostle Paul went to great lengths to show that righteousness* is a gift of God. He used the term thirty-five

---

* This includes both objective righteousness and subjective righteousness. In this book we are dealing with the issue of subjective righteousness (or sanctification if you prefer another theological term), but it is important to understand that both are gracious gifts from God. And, in fact, the Bible does not make the clear division between objective and subjective righteousness which theologians are accustomed to draw, simply because the biblical writers would find it ludicrous to talk of having one without the other.

times in that epistle and each time struck home the fact that righteousness is unattained and unattainable through human effort. One of the
clearest statements is Romans 5:17, ". . . those who receive the
abundance of grace and the *free gift of righteousness* [shall] reign in
life through the one man Jesus Christ." That teaching, of course, is
found not only in Romans but throughout Scripture and stands as one
of the cornerstones of the Christian faith.

The moment we grasp this breathtaking insight we are in danger of
an error in the opposite direction. We are tempted to believe there is
nothing we can do. If all human strivings end in moral bankruptcy
(and having tried it, we know it is so), and if righteousness is a
gracious gift from God (as the Bible clearly states), then is it not logi-
cal to conclude that we must wait for God to come and transform us?
Strangely enough, the answer is "no." The analysis is correct: human
striving *is* insufficient and righteousness *is* a gift from God. It is the
conclusion that is faulty, for happily there is something we can do. We
do not need to be hung on the horns of the dilemma of either human
works or idleness. God has given us the Disciplines of the spiritual life
as a means of receiving His grace. The Disciplines allow us to place
ourselves before God so that He can transform us.

The apostle Paul said, "he who sows to his own flesh will from the
flesh reap corruption; but he who sows to the Spirit will from the Spirit
reap eternal life" (Gal. 6:8). A farmer is helpless to grow grain; all he
can do is to provide the right conditions for the growing of grain. He
puts the seed in the ground where the natural forces take over and up
comes the grain. That is the way with the Spiritual Disciplines—they
are a way of sowing to the Spirit. The Disciplines are God's way of
getting us into the ground; they put us where He can work within us
and transform us. By themselves the Spiritual Disciplines can do nothing; they can only get us to the place where something can be done.
They are God's means of grace. The inner righteousness we seek is
not something that is poured on our heads. God has ordained the Disciplines of the spiritual life as the means by which we are placed
where He can bless us.

In this regard it would be proper to speak of "the way of disciplined
grace." It is "grace" because it is free; it is "disciplined" because
there is something for us to do. In *The Cost of Discipleship* Dietrich
Bonhoeffer made clear that grace is free, but it is not cheap. Once we

clearly understand that God's grace is unearned and unearnable, and if we expect to grow, we must take up a consciously chosen course of action involving both individual and group life. That is the purpose of the Spiritual Disciplines.

It might be helpful to visualize what we have been discussing. Picture a narrow ledge with a sheer drop-off on either side. The chasm to the right is the way of moral bankruptcy through human strivings for righteousness. Historically this has been called the heresy of moralism. The chasm to the left is the way of moral bankruptcy through the absence of human strivings. This has been called the heresy of antinomianism. On the ledge there is a path, the Disciplines of the spiritual life. This path leads to the inner transformation and healing for which we seek. We must never veer off to the right or the left, but stay on the path. The path is fraught with severe difficulties, but also with incredible joys. As we travel on this path, the blessing of God will come upon us and reconstruct us into the image of His Son Jesus Christ. We must always remember that the path does not produce the change; it only puts us in the place where the change can occur. This is the way of disciplined grace.

There is a saying in moral theology that "virtue is easy." It is true only to the extent that God's gracious work has taken over our inner spirit and transformed the ingrained habit patterns of our lives. Until that is accomplished, virtue is hard, very hard indeed. We struggle to exhibit a loving and compassionate spirit, yet it is as if we are bringing something in from the outside. Then bubbling up from the inner depths is the one thing we did not want, a biting and bitter spirit. However, once we have lived in the way of disciplined grace for a season, we discover internal changes.

We did no more than receive a gift, yet we know the changes are real. We know they are real because we find that the spirit of compassion we once found so hard is now easy. In fact, the hard thing would be to be full of bitterness. Divine Love has entered our inner spirit and taken over our habit patterns. In the unguarded moments there is a spontaneous flow from the inner sanctuary of our lives of "love, joy, peace, patience, kindness, goodness, faithfulness, gentleness, self-control" (Gal. 5:22, 23). No longer is there the tiring need to hide our inner selves from others. We do not have to work at being good and kind; we *are* good and kind. It would be work to refrain from being good and kind, because goodness and kindness are part of our nature. Just as the natural motions of our lives once produced mire and dirt, now they produce the fruit of the Spirit. Shakespeare once wrote, "The quality of mercy is not strained"—nor are any of the spiritual virtues once they have taken over the personality.

The Way of Death: Turning the Disciplines into Laws

The Spiritual Disciplines are intended for our good. They are meant to bring the abundance of God into our lives. It is possible, however, to turn them into another set of soul-killing laws. Law-bound Disciplines breathe death.

Jesus taught that we must go beyond the righteousness of the scribes and the Pharisees (Mt. 5:20). Yet we need to see that their righteousness was no small thing. They were committed to following God in a way that many of us are not prepared to do. One factor, however, was always central to their righteousness: *externalism*. Their righteousness consisted in control over externals, often including the manipulation of others. The extent to which we have gone beyond the righteousness of the scribes and the Pharisees is seen in how much our lives demonstrate the internal work of God upon the heart. It will have external results, but the work will be internal. It is easy in our zeal for the Spiritual Disciplines to turn them into the external righteousness of the scribes and the Pharisees.

When the Disciplines degenerate into law, they are used to manipulate and control people. We take explicit commands and use them to imprison others. The result of such deterioration of the Spiritual Disciplines is pride and fear. Pride takes over because we come to believe that we are the right kind of people. Fear takes over because the power of controlling others carries with it the anxiety of losing control, and the anxiety of being controlled by others.

If we are to progress in the spiritual walk so that the Disciplines are a blessing and not a curse, we must come to the place in our lives where we lay down the everlasting burden of needing to manage others. That need more than any single thing will lead us to turn the Spiritual Disciplines into laws. Once we have made a law, we have an "externalism" by which we can judge who is measuring up and who is not. Without laws the Disciplines are primarily an internal work and it is impossible to control an internal work. When we genuinely believe that inner transformation is God's work and not ours, we can put to rest our passion to set others straight.

We must beware of how quickly we can latch onto this word or that word and turn it into a law. The moment we do so we qualify for Jesus' stern pronouncement against the Pharisees: "They bind heavy burdens, hard to bear, and lay them on men's shoulders; but they themselves will not move them with their finger" (Mt. 23:4). In these matters we need the words of the apostle Paul embedded in our minds: "We deal not in the letter but in the Spirit. The letter of the Law leads to the death of the soul; the Spirit of God alone can give life to the soul" (2 Cor. 3:6, Phillips).

As we enter the inner world of the Spiritual Disciplines, there will always be the danger of turning them into laws. But we are not left to our own human devices. Jesus Christ has promised to be our present Teacher and Guide. His voice is not hard to hear. His instruction is not hard to understand. If we are beginning to calcify what should always remain alive and growing, He will tell us. We can trust His teaching. If we are wandering off toward some wrong idea or unprofitable practice, He will guide us back. If we are willing to listen to the Heavenly Monitor, we will receive the instruction we need.

Our world is hungry for genuinely changed people. Leo Tolstoy observed, "Everybody thinks of changing humanity and nobody thinks of changing himself." [9] Let us be among those who believe that the inner transformation of our lives is a goal worthy of our best effort.

PART I

The Inward Disciplines

2. THE DISCIPLINE OF MEDITATION

True contemplation is not a psychological trick but a theological grace.—Thomas Merton

In contemporary society our Adversary majors in three things: noise, hurry, and crowds. If he can keep us engaged in "muchness" and "manyness," he will rest satisfied. Psychiatrist C. G. Jung once remarked, "Hurry is not *of* the Devil; it *is* the Devil." [1]

If we hope to move beyond the superficialities of our culture— including our religious culture—we must be willing to go down into the recreating silences, into the inner world of contemplation. In their writings, all of the masters of meditation strive to awaken us to the fact that the universe is much larger than we know, that there are vast unexplored inner regions that are just as real as the physical world we know so well. They tell us of exciting possibilities for new life and freedom. They call us to the adventure, to be pioneers in this frontier of the Spirit. Though it may sound strange to modern ears, we should without shame enroll as apprentices in the school of contemplative prayer.

Understandable Misconceptions

Often there is a question as to whether meditation can be spoken of as Christian. Is it not rather the exclusive property of Eastern religions? Whenever I speak to a group on meditation as a classic Christian Discipline, there is the inevitable raising of eyebrows. "I thought TM was the group that dealt with meditation." "Don't tell me you are going to give us a mantra to recite!"

It is a sad commentary on the spiritual state of modern Christianity that meditation is a word so foreign to its ears. Meditation has always stood as a classical and central part of Christian devotion, a crucial preparation for and adjunct to the work of prayer. No doubt part of the surge of interest in Eastern meditation is because the churches have abrogated the field. How depressing for a university student, seeking to know the Christian teaching on meditation, to discover that there are so few living masters of contemplative prayer and that nearly all of the serious writings on the subject are seven or more centuries old. No wonder he or she turns to Zen, Yoga, or TM.

Meditation was certainly not foreign to the authors of Scripture. "And Isaac went out to meditate in the field in the evening" (Gen. 24:63). "I think of thee upon my bed, and meditate on thee in the watches of the night" (Ps. 63:6). These were people who were close to the heart of God. God spoke to them not because they had special abilities, but because they were willing to listen. The Psalms virtually sing of the meditations of the people of God upon the law of God: "My eyes are awake before the watches of the night, that I may meditate upon thy promise" (Ps. 119:148). The psalm which introduces the entire Psalter calls all people to emulate the "blessed man" whose "delight is in the law of the Lord, and on his law he meditates day and night" (Ps. 1:2).

Christian writers throughout the centuries have spoken of a way of listening to God, of communing with the Creator of heaven and earth, of experiencing the Eternal Lover of the world. Such fine thinkers as Augustine, Francis of Assisi, François Fénelon, Madame Guyon, Bernard of Clairvaux, Francis de Sales, Juliana of Norwich, Brother Lawrence, George Fox, John Woolman, Evelyn Underhill, Thomas Merton, Frank Laubach, Thomas Kelly and many others speak of this more excellent way.

Scripture tells us that John was "in the Spirit on the Lord's day" when he received his apocalyptic vision (Rev. 1:10). Could it be that John was trained in a way of listening and seeing that we have forgotten? R. D. Laing writes, "We live in a secular world. . . . There is a prophecy in Amos that a time will come when there will be a famine in the land, 'not a famine for bread, nor a thirst for water, but of hearing the words of the Lord.' That time has now come to pass. It is the present age." [2]

Let us have the courage to side with the biblical tradition and once again learn the ancient (and yet contemporary) art of meditation. May we join with the psalmist and declare, "As for me, I will meditate on thy precepts" (Ps. 119:78).

Then there are those who feel that the Christian idea of meditation is synonymous with the concept of meditation centered in Eastern religion. In reality they stand worlds apart. Eastern meditation is an attempt to empty the mind; Christian meditation is an attempt to empty the mind in order to fill it. The two ideas are radically different.

All Eastern forms of meditation stress the need to become detached from the world. There is an emphasis upon losing personhood and individuality and merging with the Cosmic Mind. There is a longing to be released from the burdens and pains of this life and be caught up into the effortless, suspended bliss of Nirvana. Personal identity is lost in a pool of cosmic consciousness. Detachment is the final goal of Eastern religion. It is an escaping from the miserable wheel of existence. There is no God to be attached to or to hear from. Zen and Yoga are popular forms of this approach. Transcendental Meditation has the same Buddhist roots but in its Western form is something of an aberration. In its popular form, TM is meditation for the materialist. You do not need to believe in the spiritual realm in the least to practice it. It is merely a method of controlling the brain waves in order to improve your physiological and emotional well-being. More advanced forms of TM do involve the spiritual nature, and then it takes on exactly the same characteristics as all other Eastern religions.

Christian meditation goes far beyond the notion of detachment. There is need for detachment—"sabbath of contemplation" as Peter of Celles, a Benedictine monk of the twelfth century, put it.[3] But we must go on to *attachment*. The detachment from the confusion all around us is in order to have a richer attachment to God and to other human beings. Christian meditation leads us to the inner wholeness necessary to give ourselves to God freely, and to the spiritual perception necessary to attack social evils. In this sense it is the most practical of all the Disciplines.

There is a danger in thinking only in terms of detachment, as Jesus indicated in His story of the man who had been emptied of evil but not filled with good. "When the unclean spirit has gone out of a man . . . he goes and brings seven other spirits more evil than himself, and they enter and dwell there; and the last state of that man becomes worse than the first" (Lk. 11:24–26).[4]

Some shy away from meditation out of fear that it is too difficult, too complicated. Perhaps it is best left to the professional who has more time to explore the inner regions. Not at all. The acknowledged experts in this way never report that they are on a journey only for the privileged few, the spiritual giants. They would laugh at the very idea. They felt that what they were doing was a natural human activity—as natural, and as important, as breathing. They would tell us that we do not need any special gifts or psychic powers. All we need to do is discipline and train latent faculties within us. Anyone who can tap the power of the imagination can learn to meditate. If we are capable of listening to our dreams, we are taking the first steps. Thomas Merton, one who ought to know, wrote, "Meditation is really very simple; there is not much need to elaborate techniques to teach us how to go about it."[5]

So that we may not be led astray, however, we must understand that we are not engaging in some flippant work. We are not calling on some cosmic bellhop. It is serious and even dangerous business. It should demand our best thought and energies. No one should undertake meditation merely for diversion or because others are doing it. Those who enter into it halfheartedly will certainly fail. P. T. Rohrbach has written, "The best over-all preparation for successful meditation is a personal conviction of its importance and a staunch determination to persevere in its practice."[6] Like any serious work, it is more difficult in the apprentice stages; once we are skilled—journeymen—it is part of our ingrained habit patterns. "Waiting upon God is not idleness," said Bernard of Clairvaux, "but work which beats all other work to one unskilled in it."[7]

Then there are those who view the way of contemplation as impractical and wholly out of touch with the twentieth century. There is a fear it will lead to the kind of person Dostoevski immortalized in his book *The Brothers Karamazov* in the ascetic Father Ferapont: a rigid, self-righteous person who by sheer effort delivers himself from the world, and then calls down curses upon it. At its very best, such meditation would lead to an unhealthy other worldliness that keeps us immune to the suffering of humanity.

Such evaluations are far off the mark. In fact, meditation is the one thing that can sufficiently redirect our lives so that we can deal with human life successfully. Thomas Merton wrote, "Meditation has no point and no reality unless it is firmly rooted in *life*." [8] Historically, no group has stressed the need to enter into the listening silences more than the Quakers and the result has been a vital social impact far in excess of their numbers. The contemplatives themselves were men and women of action. Meister Eckhart wrote, "Even if a man were in rapture like St. Paul and knew a man who was in need of food he would do better by feeding him than by remaining in ecstasy." [9]

Often meditation will yield insights that are deeply practical, almost mundane. There will come instruction on how to relate to your wife or husband, on how to deal with this sensitive problem or that business situation. More than once I have received guidance on what attitude to have when lecturing in a college classroom. It is wonderful when a particular meditation leads to ecstasy, but it is far more common to be given guidance in dealing with ordinary human problems. Morton Kelsey has said:

> What we do with our lives outwardly, how well we care for others, is as much a part of meditation as what we do in the quietness and turning inward. In fact, Christian meditation that does not make a difference in the quality of one's outer life is short-circuited. It may flare for a while, but unless it results in finding richer and more loving relationships with other human beings or in changing conditions in the world that cause human suffering, the chances are that an individual's prayer activity will fizzle out.[10]

Perhaps the most common misconception of all is to view meditation as a religious form of psychological manipulation. It may have value in dropping our blood pressure or in relieving tension. It may even provide us with meaningful insights by helping us get in touch with our subconscious mind. But the idea of actual contact and communion with a spiritual sphere of existence sounds unscientific and faintly unreasonable. If you feel that we live in a purely physical universe, you will view meditation as a good way to obtain a consistent alpha brain-wave pattern. (TM attempts to project exactly this image, which makes it highly appealing to modern secular men and women.) But if you believe that we live in a universe created by the infinite-personal God who delights in our communion with Him, you will see meditation as a communication between the Lover and the one beloved. As Albert the Great said, "The contemplation of the saints is fired by the love of the one contemplated: that is, God." [11]

These two concepts of meditation are complete opposites. The one confines us to a totally human experience, the other catapults us into a divine-human encounter. The one talks about the exploration of the subconscious, the other speaks of "resting in him whom we have *found,* who loves us, who is near to us, who comes to us to draw us to himself." [12] Both may sound religious and even use religious jargon, but the former can ultimately find no place for spiritual reality.

How then do we come to believe in a world of the spirit? Is it by blind faith? Not at all. The inner reality of the spiritual world is available to all who are willing to search for it. Often I have discovered that those who so freely debunk the spiritual world have never taken ten minutes to investigate whether or not such a world really exists. Like any other scientific endeavor, we form a hypothesis and experiment with it to see if it is true or not. If our first experiment fails, we do not despair or label the whole business fraudulent. We reexamine our procedure, perhaps adjust our hypothesis and try again. We should at least have the honesty to persevere in this work to the same degree we would in any field of science. The fact that so many are unwilling to do so betrays not their intelligence but their prejudice.

Desiring the Living Voice of God

There are times when everything within us says "yes" to these lines of Frederick W. Faber:

> Only to sit and think of God,
>   Oh what a joy it is!
> To think the thought, to breathe the Name
>   Earth has no higher bliss. [13]

But those who meditate know that the more frequent reaction is spiritual inertia, a coldness and lack of desire. Human beings seem to have a perpetual tendency to have somebody else talk to God for them. We

are content to have the message secondhand. At Sinai the people cried
out to Moses, "You speak to us, and we will hear; but let not God
speak to us, lest we die" (Ex. 20:19). One of the fatal mistakes of
Israel was their insistence upon having a human king rather than resting in the theocratic rule of God over them. We can detect a note of
sadness in the word of the Lord, "They have rejected me from being
king over them" (1 Sam. 8:7). The history of religion is the story of
an almost desperate scramble to have a king, a mediator, a priest, a
go-between. In this way we do not need to go to God ourselves. Such
an approach saves us from the need to change, for to be in the presence of God is to change. It is very convenient this way because it
gives us the advantage of religious respectability without demanding
moral transformation. We do not need to observe the American scene
very closely to realize that it is captivated by the religion of the mediator.

That is why meditation is so threatening to us. It boldly calls us to
enter into the living presence of God for ourselves. It tells us that God
is speaking in the continuous present and wants to address us. Jesus
and the New Testament writers make clear that this is not just for the
religious professionals—the priests—but for everyone. *All* who acknowledge Jesus Christ as Lord *are* the universal priesthood of God
and as such can enter the Holy of Holies and converse with the living
God.

It seems so difficult to bring people to believe that *they* can hear
God's voice. Members of the Church of the Saviour in Washington,
D.C., have been experimenting in this field for some time. Their
conclusion: "We think that we are twentieth- and twenty-first-century
people; nonetheless, we have hints that one can receive directions as
clear as those given Ananias, . . . 'Rise and go to the street called
straight.' " [14] Why not? If God is alive and active in the affairs of
human beings, why can't His voice be heard and obeyed today? It can
and is heard by all who will know Him as present Teacher and
Prophet.

How do we receive the desire to hear His voice? "This desire to
turn is a gift of grace. Anyone who imagines he can simply begin
meditating without praying for the desire and the grace to do so, will
soon give up. But the desire to meditate, and the grace to begin medi-

tating, should be taken as an implicit promise of further graces."[15] Seeking and receiving that "gift of grace" is the only thing that will keep us moving forward on the inward journey.

Preparing to Meditate

It is impossible to learn how to meditate from a book. We learn to meditate by meditating. Simple suggestions at the right time, however, can make an immense difference. The practical hints and meditation exercises on the following pages are given in the hope that they may help in the actual practice of meditation. They are not laws nor are they intended to confine you; rather, they are a few of the many windows into the inward world.

When a certain proficiency has been attained in the interior life, it is possible to practice meditation nearly anywhere and under almost every circumstance. Brother Lawrence in the seventeenth century and Thomas Kelly in the twentieth both bear eloquent testimony to that fact. Having said that, however, we must see the importance for beginners and proficients alike to give some part of each day to formal meditation. If untold thousands can take twenty minutes twice a day to recite a mantra, we should have no less dedication to stated times for meditation.

Once we are convinced that we need to set aside specific times for contemplation, we must guard against the notion that to do certain religious acts at particular times means that we are finally meditating. This work involves all of life. It is a twenty-four-hour-a-day job. Contemplative prayer is a way of life. "Pray without ceasing," Paul exhorted (1 Thess. 5:17, KJV). With a touch of humor Peter of Celles noted that "he who snores in the night of vice cannot know the light of contemplation."[16]

We must come to see, therefore, how central the whole of our day is in preparing us for specific times of meditation. If we are constantly being swept off our feet with frantic activity, we will be unable to be attentive at the moment of inward silence. A mind that is harassed and fragmented by external affairs is hardly prepared for meditation. The church Fathers often spoke of *Otium Sanctum:* "holy leisure." It refers to a sense of balance in the life, an ability to be at peace through the activities of the day, an ability to rest and take time to enjoy beauty, an ability to pace ourselves. With our tendency to define people in terms of what they produce, we would do well to cultivate "holy leisure." And if we expect to succeed in the contemplative arts, we must pursue "holy leisure" with a determination that is ruthless to our datebooks.

What about a *place* for meditation? This will be discussed in detail under the Discipline of Solitude; for now a few words will be sufficient. Find a place that is quiet and free from interruption. There should be no telephone nearby. If it is possible to have a place that looks out onto trees or plants, so much the better. It is best to have one designated place rather than hunting for a different spot each day.

What about *posture?* In one sense posture makes no difference at all; you can pray anywhere, any time, and in any position. In another sense, however, posture is of utmost importance. The body, the mind and the spirit are inseparable. Tension in the spirit is telegraphed in body language. I have actually witnessed people go through an entire worship service continuously chewing gum, without the slightest awareness of their deep inner tension. Not only does outward posture reflect the inward state, it can also help to nurture the inner attitude of prayer. If inwardly we are fraught with distractions and anxiety, a consciously chosen posture of peace and relaxation will have a tendency to calm our inner turmoil.

There is no "law" that prescribes a correct posture. The Bible contains everything from lying prostrate on the floor to standing with hands and head lifted toward the heavens. The lotus position of Eastern religion is simply another example—not a law—of posture. The best approach would be to find a position that is the most comfortable and the least distracting. The delightful fourteenth-century mystic, Richard Rolle, favored sitting, ". . . because I knew that I . . . longer lasted . . . than going, or standing or kneeling. For [in] sitting I am most at rest, and my heart most upward." [17] I quite agree, and find it best to sit in a straight chair, with the back correctly positioned in the chair and both feet flat on the floor. To slouch indicates inattention and to cross the legs restricts the circulation. Place the hands on the knees, palms up in a gesture of receptivity. Sometimes it is good to close the eyes in order to remove distractions and center the attention on the living Christ. At other times it is helpful to ponder a picture of the Lord or look out at the lovely trees and plants for the same purpose. Regardless of how it is done, the aim is to center the attention of the body, the emotions, the mind and the spirit upon "the glory of God in the face of Christ" (2 Cor. 4:6).

How to Meditate—First Steps

The inner world of meditation is most easily entered through the door of the imagination. We fail today to appreciate its tremendous power. The imagination is stronger than conceptual thought and stronger than the will. In the West, our tendency to deify the merits of rationalism— and it does have merit—has caused us to ignore the value of the imagination.

Some rare individuals may be able to contemplate in an imageless void, but most of us need to be more deeply rooted in the senses. Jesus taught this way, making constant appeal to the imagination and the senses. In *Introduction to the Devout Life,* Francis de Sales wrote:

> By means of the imagination we confine our mind within the mystery on which we meditate, that it may not ramble to and fro, just as we shut up a bird in a cage or tie a hawk by his leash so that he may rest on the hand. Some may perhaps tell you that it is better to use the simple thought of faith and to conceive the subject in a manner entirely mental and spiritual in the representation of the mysteries, or else to imagine that the things take place in your own soul. This method is too subtle for beginners.[18]

We simply must become convinced of the importance of thinking and experiencing in images. It came so spontaneously to us as children, but for years now we have been trained to disregard the imagination, even to fear it. In his autobiography C. G. Jung describes how difficult it was for him to humble himself and once again play the imagination games of a child, and the value of that experience. Just as children need to learn to think logically, adults need to rediscover the magical reality of the imagination.

Ignatius of Loyola in his *Spiritual Exercises* constantly encouraged his readers to visualize the Gospel stories. Every contemplation he gave was designed to open up the imagination. He even included a meditation entitled "application of the senses," which is an attempt to help us utilize all five senses as we picture the Gospel events. His thin volume of meditation exercises with its stress on the imagination had tremendous impact for good upon the sixteenth century.*

In learning to meditate, one good place to begin is with our dreams, since it involves little more than paying attention to something we are already doing. For fifteen centuries Christians overwhelmingly considered dreams as a natural way in which the spiritual world broke into our lives. Kelsey, who has authored the book *Dreams: The Dark Speech of the Spirit,* notes, ". . . every major Father of the early Church, from Justin Martyr to Irenaeus, from Clement and Tertullian to Origen and Cyprian, believed that dreams were a means of revelation."[19]

With the rationalism of the Renaissance came a certain skepticism about dreams. Then in the formative days of the development of psychology, Freud stressed mainly the negative side of dreams, since he worked almost entirely with mental illness. Hence, modern men and women have tended either to ignore dreams altogether, or to fear that an interest in them will lead to neurosis. It does not need to be so; and, in fact, if we will listen, dreams can help us find increased maturity and health.

If we are convinced that dreams can be a key to unlocking the door to the inner world, we can do three practical things. First, we can specifically pray, inviting God to inform us through our dreams. We should tell Him of our willingness to allow Him to speak to us in this way. At the same time, it is wise to pray a prayer of protection, since to open ourselves to spiritual influence can be dangerous as well as profitable. We simply ask God to surround us with the light of His protection as He ministers to our spirit.

Second, we should begin to record our dreams. People do not remember their dreams, because they do not pay attention to them. Keeping a journal of our dreams is a way of taking them seriously. It is, of course, foolish to view every dream as deeply significant or as some revelation from God. The only thing more foolish is to view all dreams as only chaotic and irrational. In the recording of dreams, certain patterns begin to emerge and insights come. It is not long before it

---

* See *The Spiritual Exercises of St. Ignatius,* trans. Anthony Mottola (New York: Doubleday & Company, 1964). If kept from becoming dogmatically rigid, these are delightful meditations.

is easy to distinguish between significant dreams and those that are the result of having seen the late show the night before.

That leads to the third consideration—how to interpret dreams. The best way to discover the meaning of dreams is to *ask*. "You do not have, because you do not ask" (Jas. 4:2). We can trust God to bring discernment if and when it is needed. Sometimes it is helpful to seek out those who are especially skilled in these matters. Benedict Pererius, a sixteenth-century Jesuit, suggested that the best interpreter of dreams is the ". . . person with plenty of experience in the world and the affairs of humanity, with a wide interest in everything human, and who is open to the voice of God."[20]

How to Meditate—Specific Exercises

There is a progression in the spiritual life. It is not wise to tackle the Mt. Everest of the soul before having had some experience with lesser peaks. So I would recommend beginning with a daily period of from five to ten minutes. This time is for learning to "center down," or what the contemplatives of the Middle Ages called "re-collection." It is a time to become still, to enter into the recreating silence, to allow the fragmentation of our minds to become centered.

The following are two brief exercises that will aid you in "centering down." The first one is simply called "palms down, palms up." Begin by placing your palms down as a symbolic indication of your desire to turn over any concerns you may have to God. Inwardly you may pray "Lord, I give to You my anger toward John. I release my fear of my dentist appointment this morning. I surrender my anxiety over not having enough money to pay the bills this month. I release my frustration over trying to find a baby-sitter for tonight." Whatever it is that weighs on your mind or is a concern to you, just say, "palms down." Release it. You may even feel a certain sense of release in your hands. After several moments of surrender, turn your palms up as a symbol of your desire to receive from the Lord. Perhaps you will pray silently: "Lord, I would like to receive Your divine Love for John, Your peace about the dentist appointment, Your patience, Your joy." Whatever you need, you say, "palms up." Having centered down, spend the remaining moments in complete silence. Do not ask for anything. Allow the Lord to commune with your spirit, to love you. If impressions or directions come, fine; if not, fine.

Another meditation aimed at centering oneself begins by concentrating on breathing. Having seated yourself comfortably, slowly become conscious of your breathing. This will help you to get in touch with your body and indicate to you the level of tension within. Inhale deeply, slowly tilting your head back as far as it will go. Then exhale, allowing your head slowly to come forward until your chin nearly rests on your chest. Do this for several moments, praying inwardly something like this: "Lord, I exhale my fear over my geometry exam, I inhale Your peace. I exhale my spiritual apathy, I inhale Your light and life." Then, as before, become silent outwardly and inwardly. Be attentive to the inward living Christ. If your attention wanders to the letter that must be dictated, or the windows that need to be cleaned, "exhale" the matter into the arms of the Master and draw in His divine breath of peace. Then listen once again.

At the end of each meditation, close with a genuine expression of thanksgiving.

After you have gained some proficiency in centering down, add a five- to ten-minute meditation on some aspect of the creation. Choose something in the created order: tree, plant, bird, leaf, cloud, and each day ponder it carefully and prayerfully. God who made the heavens and the earth uses His creation to show us something of His glory and give us something of His life. "The simplest and oldest way . . . in which God manifests Himself is . . . through and in the earth itself. And He still speaks to us through the earth and the sea, the birds of the air and the little living creatures upon the earth, if we can but quiet ourselves to listen." [21] We should not bypass this means of God's grace, for as Evelyn Underhill warns:

> To elude nature, to refuse her friendship, and attempt to leap the river of life in the hope of finding God on the other side, is the common error of a perverted mysticality. . . . So you are to begin with that first form of contemplation which the old mystics sometimes called the "discovery of God in His creatures." [22]

Having practiced for some weeks with the two kinds of meditation listed above, you will want to add the meditation upon Scripture. Like the hub of a wheel, the meditation upon Scripture becomes the central reference point by which all other meditations are kept in proper perspective. The *meditatio Scripturarum* is considered by all the masters as the normal foundation for the interior life. Whereas the study of Scripture centers on exegesis, the meditation of Scripture centers on internalizing and personalizing the passage. The written Word becomes a living word addressed to you.

Take a single event like the resurrection, or a parable, or a few verses, or even a single word and allow it to take root in you. Seek to live the experience, remembering the encouragement of Ignatius of Loyola to apply all our senses to our task. Smell the sea. Hear the lap of water along the shore. See the crowd. Feel the sun on your head and the hunger in your stomach. Taste the salt in the air. Touch the hem of His garment. Francis de Sales has instructed us to

> . . . represent to your imagination the whole of the mystery on which you desire to meditate as if it really passed in your presence. For example, if you wish to meditate on our Lord on the Cross, imagine that you are on Mount Calvary, and that you there behold and hear all that was done or said on the day of the Passion.[23]

As you enter the story, not as a passive observer but as an active participant, remember that since Jesus lives in the Eternal Now and is not bound by time, this event in the past is a living present-tense experience for Him. Hence, you can *actually* encounter the living Christ in the event, be addressed by His voice and be touched by His healing power. It can be more than an exercise of the imagination; it can be a genuine confrontation. Jesus Christ will actually come to you.

This is not a time for technical word studies, or analysis, or even the gathering of material to share with others. Set aside all tendencies toward arrogance and with a humble heart receive the Word addressed to you. Often I find kneeling especially appropriate for this particular time. Dietrich Bonhoeffer said, ". . . just as you do not analyze the words of someone you love, but accept them as they are said to you, accept the Word of Scripture and ponder it in your heart, as Mary did. That is all. That is meditation."[24] When Bonhoeffer founded the seminary at Finkenwalde, a one-half hour silent meditation upon Scripture was corporately agreed upon and practiced by all the seminarians and faculty.

It is important to resist the temptation to pass over many passages superficially. Our rushing reflects our internal state and our internal state is what needs to be transformed. Bonhoeffer recommended spending a whole week on a single text! In addition, you will want to live with your chosen Scripture throughout the day.*

A fourth form of meditation has as its objective to bring you into a deep inner communion with the Father where you look at Him and He looks at you. In your imagination, picture yourself walking along a lovely forest path. Take your time, allowing the blaring noise of our modern megalopolis to be overtaken by the sound of rustling leaves and cool forest streams. After observing yourself for a bit, take the perspective of the one walking, rather than the one observed. Try to feel the breeze upon your face as if it were gently blowing away all anxiety. Stop along the way to ponder the beauty of flowers and birds. When you are able to experience the scene with all your senses, the path breaks out onto a lovely grassy knoll. Walk out into the lush large meadow encircled by stately pines. After exploring the meadow for a time, lie down on your back looking up at blue sky and white clouds. Enjoy the sights and smells. Thank the Lord for the beauty.

After awhile there is a deep yearning within to go into the upper regions beyond the clouds. In your imagination allow your spiritual body, shining with light, to rise out of your physical body. Look back so that you can see yourself lying in the grass and reassure your body that you will return momentarily. Imagine your spiritual self, alive and vibrant, rising up through the clouds and into the stratosphere. Observe your physical body, the knoll, and the forest shrink as you leave the earth. Go deeper and deeper into outer space until there is nothing except the warm presence of the eternal Creator. Rest in His presence. Listen quietly, anticipating the unanticipated. Note carefully any instruction given. With time and experience you will be able to distin-

---

* Space hinders detailed meditations on Scripture. In *The Other Side of Silence,* Kelsey provides over sixty pages of specific meditations. *The Spiritual Exercises* of Ignatius of Loyola is another resource. Also Lyman Coleman has written a number of "Serendipity" study books, published by Word, Inc., whose aim is to aid you in *experiencing* the biblical passage.

guish readily between mere human thought that may bubble up to the conscious mind and the True Spirit which inwardly moves upon the heart. Do not be surprised if the instruction is terribly practical and not in the least what you thought of as "spiritual." Do not be disappointed if no words come; like good friends, you are silently enjoying the company of each other. When it is time for you to leave, audibly thank the Lord for His goodness and return to the meadow. Walk joyfully back along the path until you return home full of new life and energy.*

There is a fifth form of meditation which is in some ways quite the opposite of the one just given. It is to meditate upon the events of our time and to seek to perceive their significance. We have a spiritual obligation to penetrate the inner meaning of events and political pressures, not to gain power, but to gain prophetic perspective. Thomas Merton said that the person

> . . . who has meditated on the Passion of Christ but has not meditated on the extermination camps of Dachau and Auschwitz has not yet fully entered into the experience of Christianity in our time. . . . Indeed, the contemplative above all should ruminate on these terrible realities which are so symptomatic, so important, so prophetic.[25]

This form of meditation is best accomplished with the Bible in one hand and the newspaper in the other! You must not, however, be controlled by the absurd political clichés and propaganda fed us today. Actually newspapers are generally far too shallow and slanted to be of much help. We would do well to hold the events of our time before God and ask for prophetic insight to discern where these things lead. Further, we should ask for guidance for anything we personally should be doing to be salt and light in our decaying and dark world.

You must not be discouraged if in the beginning your meditations have no meaning to you. You are learning an art for which you have received no training. Nor does our culture encourage you to develop

---

* Another very enjoyable meditation entitled "pull the plugs" has the same purpose in mind and is described by Jo Kimmel in Chapter One of her book *Steps to Prayer Power* published by Abingdon Press. I have used this meditation numerous times with real profit.

these skills. You will be going against the tide, but take heart; your task is of immense worth.

There are many other aspects of the Discipline of Meditation that could have been profitably considered.* However, meditation is not a single act, nor can it be completed the way one completes the building of a chair. It is a way of life. You will be constantly learning and growing as you plumb the inner depths.

* Two topics that closely impinge upon meditation will be discussed under the Discipline of Solitude: the creative use of silence, and the concept developed by St. John of the Cross which he graphically calls "the dark night of the soul."

3. THE DISCIPLINE OF PRAYER

I am the ground of thy beseeching; first, it is my will thou shalt have it; after, I make thee to will it; and after I make thee to beseech it and thou beseechest it. How should it then be that thou shouldst not have thy beseeching?
—Juliana of Norwich

Prayer catapults us onto the frontier of the spiritual life. It is original research in unexplored territory. Meditation introduces us to the inner life, fasting is an accompanying means, but it is the Discipline of prayer itself that brings us into the deepest and highest work of the human spirit. Real prayer is life creating and life changing. "Prayer—secret, fervent, believing prayer—lies at the root of all personal godliness," [1] writes William Carey.

To pray is to change. Prayer is the central avenue God uses to transform us. If we are unwilling to change, we will abandon prayer as a noticeable characteristic of our lives. The closer we come to the heartbeat of God the more we see our need and the more we desire to be conformed to Christ. William Blake tells us that our task in life is to learn to bear God's "beams of love." How often we fashion cloaks of evasion—beam-proof shelters—in order to elude our Eternal Lover. But when we pray God slowly and graciously reveals to us our hiding places, and sets us free from them.

"You ask and do not receive, because you ask wrongly, to spend it on your passions" (Jas. 4:3). To ask "rightly" involves transformed passions, total renewal. In prayer, real prayer, we begin to think God's thoughts after Him: to desire the things He desires, to love the things He loves. Progressively we are taught to see things from His point of view.

All who have walked with God have viewed prayer as the main business of their lives. The words of Mark, "And in the morning, a great while before day, he rose and went out to a lonely place, and there he prayed," stands as a commentary on the life-style of Jesus (Mk. 1:35). David's desire for God broke the self-indulgent chains of sleep: "early will I seek Thee" (Ps. 63:1, KJV). When the apostles were tempted to invest their energies in other important and necessary tasks, they determined to give themselves continually to prayer and the ministry of the Word (Acts 6:4). Martin Luther declared, "I have so much business I cannot get on without spending three hours daily in prayer." He held it as a spiritual axiom that "He that has prayed well has studied well." [2] John Wesley said, "God does nothing but in answer to prayer," [3] and backed up his conviction by devoting two hours daily to that sacred exercise. The most notable feature of David Brainerd's life was his praying. His journal is permeated with accounts of prayer, fasting and meditation. "I love to be alone in my cottage, where I can spend much time in prayer." "I set apart this day for secret fasting and prayer to God." "When I return home and give myself to meditation, prayer, and fasting. . . ." [4]

For those explorers in the frontiers of faith, prayer was no little habit tacked onto the periphery of their lives—it *was* their lives. It was the most serious work of their most productive years. William Penn testified of George Fox that "Above all he excelled in prayer. . . . The most awful, living, reverend frame I ever felt or beheld, I must say was his in prayer." [5] Adoniram Judson sought to withdraw from business and company seven times a day in order to engage in the holy work of prayer. He began at midnight and again at dawn; then at nine, twelve, three, six and nine at night he would give time to secret prayer. John Hyde of India made prayer such a dominant characteristic of his life that he was nicknamed "Praying Hyde." For these, and all those who have braved the depths of the interior life, to breathe was to pray.

Many of us, however, are discouraged rather than challenged by such examples. Those "giants of the faith" are so far beyond anything we have experienced that we are tempted to despair. But rather than flagellating ourselves for our obvious lack, we should remember that God always meets us where we are and slowly moves us along into deeper things. Occasional joggers do not suddenly enter an Olympic marathon. They prepare and train themselves over a period of time, and so should we. When such a progression is followed, we can expect to pray with greater authority and spiritual success a year from now than at present.

It is easy for us to be defeated at the outset because we have been taught that everything in the universe is already set, and so things cannot be changed. We may gloomily feel this way, but the Bible does not teach that. The Bible pray-ers prayed as if their prayers could and would make an objective difference. The apostle Paul gladly announced that we are "colaborers with God" (1 Cor. 3:9); that is, we are working with God to determine the outcome of events. It is Stoicism that demands a closed universe, not the Bible. Many with their emphasis upon acquiescence and resignation to the way things are as "the will of God" are actually closer to Epictetus than to Christ. Moses was bold to pray because he believed he could change things, even God's mind. In fact, the Bible stresses so forcefully the openness of our universe that, in an anthropomorphism hard for modern ears, it speaks of God constantly changing His mind in accord with His unchanging love (i.e., Ex. 32:14; Jon. 3:10).

That comes as a genuine liberation to many of us but it also sets tremendous responsibility before us. We are working with God to determine the future! Certain things will happen in history if we pray rightly. We are to change the world by prayer. What more motivation do we need to learn this loftiest human exercise?

Prayer is such a vast and multiphase subject that we instantly recognize the impossibility of even lightly touching on all its aspects in one chapter. A myriad of genuinely good books have been written on prayer, one of the best of which is Andrew Murray's classic, *With Christ in the School of Prayer*. We would do well to read widely and experience deeply if we desire to know the ways of prayer. Since restriction often enhances clarity, this chapter will be confined to learning how to pray for other people with spiritual success. Modern men and women are so desperately in need of the help that we can provide that our best energies should be devoted to this task.

Learning to Pray

Real prayer is something we learn. The disciples asked Jesus, "Lord, teach us to pray" (Lk. 11:1). They had prayed all their lives and yet something about the quality and quantity of Jesus' praying caused them to see how little they knew about prayer. If their praying was to make any difference on the human scene, there were some things they needed to learn.

One of the liberating experiences in my life came when I understood that prayer involved a learning process. I was set free to question, to experiment, even to fail, for I knew I was learning. For years I had prayed for everything and with great intensity, but with only marginal success. But then I saw that I might possibly be doing some things wrong and could learn differently. I took the Gospels and cut out every reference to prayer and pasted them onto sheets of paper. When I could read the New Testament teaching on prayer at one sitting, I was shocked. Either the excuses and rationalizations for unanswered prayer I had been taught were wrong, or Jesus' words were wrong. I determined to learn to pray so that my experience conformed to the words of Jesus rather than trying to make His words conform to my impoverished experience.

Perhaps the most astonishing characteristic of Jesus' praying is that when He prayed for others He *never* concluded by saying "if it be Thy will." Nor did the apostles or prophets when they were praying for others. They obviously believed that they knew what the will of God was before they prayed the prayer of faith. They were so immersed in the milieu of the Holy Spirit that when they encountered a specific situation, they knew what should be done. Their praying was so positive that it often took the form of a direct, authoritative command: "Walk," "Be well," "Stand up." I saw that when praying for others there was evidently no room for indecisive, tentative, half-hoping, "if it be Thy will" prayers.

Next I sought out individuals who seemed to experience greater power and effectiveness in prayer than I, and asked them to teach me everything they knew. In addition I sought the wisdom and experience of past masters of prayer by securing and reading every good book I could find on the subject. I began studying the pray-ers of the Old Testament with new interest.

At the same time I began praying for others with an expectation that a change should and would occur. I am so grateful I did not wait until I was perfect or had everything straight before praying for others;

otherwise I would never have begun. P. T. Forsythe said, "Prayer is to religion what original research is to science." [6] I felt I was engaging in "original research" in the school of the Spirit. It was thrilling beyond description. Every seeming failure led to a new learning process. Christ was my present Teacher so that progressively His word was being confirmed in my experience, "If you abide in me, and my words abide in you, ask whatever you will, and it shall be done for you" (Jn. 15:7).

To understand that the work of prayer involves a learning process saves us from arrogantly dismissing it as false or unreal. If we turn on our television set and it does not work, we do not declare that there are no such things as television waves in the air. We assume something is wrong, something we can find and correct. We check the plug, switch, tubes, until we discover what is blocking the flow of this mysterious energy that transmits pictures through the air. We can know the problem has been found and fixed by seeing whether or not the TV works. That is the way it is with prayer. We can determine if we are praying aright if the requests come to pass. If not, we look for the "break"; perhaps we are praying wrongly, perhaps something within us needs changing, perhaps there are new principles of prayer to be learned, perhaps patience and persistence are needed. We listen, make the necessary adjustments and try again. We can know that our prayers are being answered as surely as we can know that the television set is working.

One of the most critical aspects in learning to pray for others is to get in contact with God so that His life and power can be channeled through us into others. Often we assume we are in contact when we are not. For example, dozens of radio and television programs went through your room while you read these words, but you failed to pick them up because you were not tuned to the channel. Often people will pray and pray with all the faith in the world, but nothing happens. Naturally, they were not contacting the channel. We begin praying for others by first centering down and listening to the quiet thunder of the Lord of hosts. Attuning ourselves to divine breathings is spiritual work, but without it our praying is vain repetition (Mt. 6:7). Listening to the Lord is the first thing, the second thing, and the third thing necessary for successful intercession. Søren Kierkegaard once observed: "A man prayed, and at first he thought that prayer was talking. But he became more and more quiet until in the end he realized that prayer is listening."[7]

Meditation is the necessary prelude to intercession. The work of intercession, sometimes called the prayer of faith, presupposes that the prayer of guidance is perpetually ascending to the Father. We must hear, know and obey the will of God before we pray it into the lives of others. The prayer of guidance constantly precedes and surrounds the prayer of faith.

The beginning point then in learning to pray for others is to listen for guidance. In the beginning, it is wise to set aside Aunt Susie's arthritis for which you have been praying for twenty years. In physical matters we always tend to pray for the most difficult situations first: terminal cancer or multiple sclerosis. But when we listen, we will learn the importance of beginning with smaller things like colds or earaches. Success in the small corners of life gives us authority in the larger matters. If we are still, we will learn not only who God is but how His power operates.

Sometimes we are afraid that we do not have enough faith to pray for this child or that marriage. Our fears should be put to rest, for the Bible tells us that great miracles are possible through faith the size of a tiny mustard seed. Usually the courage actually to go and pray for a person is a sign of sufficient faith. Often our lack is not faith but compassion. It seems that genuine empathy between the pray-er and the pray ee often makes the difference. We are told that Jesus was "moved with compassion" for people. Compassion was an evident feature of every healing in the New Testament. We do not pray for people as "things" but as "persons" whom we love. If we have God-given compassion and concern for others, our faith will grow and strengthen as we pray. In fact, if we genuinely love people, we desire for them far more than it is within our power to give, and that will cause us to pray.

The inner sense of compassion is one of the clearest indications from the Lord that *this* is a prayer project for you. In times of meditation there may come a rise in the heart, a compulsion to intercede, an assurance of rightness, a flow of the Spirit. This inner "yes" is the divine authorization for you to pray for the person or situation. If the idea is accompanied with a sense of heaviness, then probably you should set it aside. God will lead someone else to pray for the matter.

The Foothills of Prayer

We should never make prayer too complicated. We are prone to do so
once we understand that prayer is something we must learn. It is also
easy to yield to this temptation because the more complicated we make
prayer, the more dependent people are upon us to learn how to do it.
But Jesus taught us to come like children to a father. Openness, honesty and trust mark a child's communication with his father. There is
an intimacy between parent and child that has room for both
seriousness and laughter. Meister Eckhart noted that "The soul will
bring forth Person if God laughs into her and she laughs back to
him." [8]

Jesus taught us to pray for daily bread; a child asks for breakfast in
utter confidence that it will be provided. He has no need to stash away
today's pancakes for fear none will be available tomorrow—as far as
he is concerned, there is an endless supply of pancakes. A child does
not find it difficult or complicated to talk to his father, nor does he feel
embarrassed to bring the simplest need to his attention.

Children teach us the value of the imagination. As with meditation,
the imagination is a powerful tool in the work of prayer. We may be
reticent to pray with the imagination, feeling that it is slightly beneath
us. Children have no such reticence. Neither did St. Teresa of Avila:
"This was my method of prayer; as I could not make reflections with
my understanding, I contrived to picture Christ within me. . . . I did
many simple things of this kind. . . . I believe my soul gained very
much in this way, because I began to practice prayer without knowing
what it was." [9] In *Saint Joan,* by George Bernard Shaw, Joan of Arc
insisted that she heard voices which came from God. She was informed by skeptics that the voices came from her imagination. Unmoved Joan replied, "Yes, that is how God speaks to me."

Imagination opens the door to faith. If we can "see" in our mind's
eye a shattered marriage whole or a sick person well, it is only a short
step to believing that it will be so.* Children instantly understand

---

* I have been greatly helped in my understanding of the value of the imagination in
praying for others by Agnes Sanford and my dear friend, Pastor Bill Vaswig. Pastor
Vaswig's book, *I Prayed, He Answered* (Augsburg Publishing House, 1977) is an excellent resource for learning to pray with the imagination, and the idea for some of the
following visualizations come from this source.

these things and respond well to praying with the imagination. I was once called to a home to pray for a seriously ill baby girl. Her four-year-old brother was in the room and so I told him I needed his help to pray for his baby sister. He was delighted and so was I, since I know that children can often pray with unusual effectiveness. He climbed up into the chair beside me. "Let's play a little game," I said. "Since we know that Jesus is always with us, let's imagine that He is sitting over in the chair across from us. He is waiting patiently for us to center our attention on Him. When we see Him, we start thinking more about His love than how sick Julie is. He smiles, gets up, and comes over to us. Then let's both put our hands on Julie and when we do, Jesus will put His hands on top of ours. We'll watch and imagine that the light from Jesus is flowing right into your little sister and making her well. Let's pretend that the light of Christ fights with the bad germs until they are all gone. Okay!" Seriously the little one nodded. Together we prayed in this childlike way and then thanked the Lord that what we "saw" was the way it was going to be. Now, I do not know whether this created a posthypnotic suggestion in the child or whether it was divine fiat, but I do know that the next morning Julie was perfectly well.

Children who experience problems in the classroom respond readily to prayer. A friend of mine who taught emotionally handicapped children decided to begin praying for them. Of course, he did not tell the children what he was doing; he simply did it. When one of the children would crawl under his desk and assume a fetal position, my teacher friend would take the child in his arms and pray silently that the light and life of Christ would heal the hurt and self-hate within the boy. So as not to embarrass him, the teacher would walk around the room continuing his regular duties while he prayed. After a while the child would relax and was soon back at his desk. Sometimes my friend would ask the boy if he ever remembered what it felt like to win a race. If the boy said "yes," he would encourage him to picture himself crossing the finish line with all his friends cheering him on and loving him. In that way the child was able to cooperate in the prayer project as well as reinforce his own self-acceptance. (Is it not ironic that people will be deeply concerned over the issue of public prayer in the schools and so seldom utilize the opportunity to pray for school children in this way, against which there can be no law!)

By the end of the school year, every child but two was able to return to a regular classroom. Coincidence? Perhaps, but as Archbishop William Temple once noted, the coincidences occurred much more frequently when he prayed.

God desires that marriages be healthy, whole and permanent. You may know of marriages that are in deep trouble and need your help. Perhaps the husband is having an affair with some other woman. Consider praying once a day for thirty days for this marriage. Visualize the husband meeting the other woman and feeling dismayed and shocked that he had ever thought of getting involved with her. Watch the very thought of an illicit affair become distasteful to him. Visualize him walking in the doorway and seeing his wife and being overwhelmed with a sense of his love for her. Picture them taking a walk together and falling in love with each other as they did years ago. "See" them increasingly able to open up and talk and care. In your imagination, build a large brick wall between the husband and the other woman. Construct a home out of love and consideration for the husband and wife. Fill it with the peace of Christ.

Your pastor and the services of worship need to be bathed in prayer. Paul prayed for his people; he asked his people to pray for him. C. H. Spurgeon attributed his success to the prayers of his church. Frank Laubach told his audiences, "I am very sensitive and know whether you are praying for me. If one of you lets me down, I feel it. When you are praying for me, I feel a strange power. When *every* person in a congregation prays intensely while the pastor is preaching, a miracle happens."[10] Saturate the services of worship with your prayers. Visualize the Lord high and lifted up filling the sanctuary with His presence.

Sexual deviations can be prayed for with real assurance that a real and lasting change can occur. Sex is like a river—it is good and a wonderful blessing when kept within its proper channel. A river that overflows its banks is a dangerous thing, and so are perverted sexual drives. What are the God-created banks for sex? One man with one woman in marriage for life. It is a joy, when praying for individuals with sexual problems, to visualize a river that has overflowed its banks and invite the Lord to bring it back into its natural channel.

Your own children can and should be changed through your prayers. Pray for them in the daytime with their participation; pray for them at night when they are asleep. One delightful approach is to go into the bedroom and lightly place your hands on the sleeping child. Imagine the light of Christ flowing through your hands and healing every emotional trauma and hurt feeling your child experienced that day. Fill him or her with the peace and joy of the Lord. In sleep the child is very receptive to prayer since the conscious mind which tends to erect barriers to God's gentle influence is relaxed.

As a priest of Christ, you can perform a wonderful service by taking children into your arms and blessing them. In the Bible parents brought their children to Jesus not so that He would play with them or even teach them, but that He might lay His hands on them and bless them (Mk. 10:13–16). He has given you the ability to do the same. Blessed is the child who is blessed by adults who know how to bless!

"Flash Prayers" is an excellent idea developed by Frank Laubach in all his many books on prayer. He purposed to learn how to live so that "to *see* anybody will be to pray! To *hear* anybody, as these children talking, that boy crying, may be to pray!"[11] Flashing hard and straight prayers at people is a great thrill and can bring interesting results. I have tried it, inwardly asking the joy of the Lord and a deeper awareness of His presence to rise up within every person I meet. Sometimes people reveal no response, but other times they turn and smile as if addressed. In a bus or plane we can fancy Jesus walking down the aisles touching people on the shoulder and saying, "I love you. My greatest delight would be to forgive you and give you all good things. You have beautiful qualities still in the bud that I would unfold if only you will say 'yes.' I'd love to rule your life if you'll let me." Frank Laubach has suggested that if thousands of us would experiment with "swishing prayers" at everyone we meet and would share the results, we could learn a great deal about how to pray for others. We could change the whole atmosphere of a nation if thousands of us would constantly throw a cloak of prayer around everyone in our circle of nearness. "Units of prayer combined, like drops of water, make an ocean which defies resistance."[12]

We must never wait until we *feel* like praying before we will pray for others. Prayer is like any other work; we may not feel like working, but once we have been at it for a bit, we begin to feel like working. We may not feel like practicing the piano, but once we play for a while we feel like doing it. In the same way, our prayer muscles need to be limbered up a bit and once the blood-flow of intercession begins, we will find that we feel like praying.

We need not worry that this work will take up too much of our time, for "It takes no time, but it occupies all our time." [13] It is not prayer in addition to work, but prayer simultaneous with work. We precede, enfold, and follow all our work with prayer. Prayer and action become wedded. Thomas Kelly experienced this way of living:

> There is a way of ordering our mental life on more than one level at once. On one level we may be thinking, discussing, seeing, calculating, meeting all the demands of external affairs. But deep within, behind the scenes, at a profounder level, we may also be in prayer and adoration, song and worship, and a gentle receptiveness to divine breathings. [14]

We have so much to learn, so far to go. Certainly the yearning of our hearts is summed up by Archbishop Tait when he said, "I want a life of greater, deeper, truer prayer." [15]

4. THE DISCIPLINE OF FASTING

Some have exalted religious fasting beyond all Scripture and reason; and others have utterly disregarded it.
—John Wesley

In a culture where the landscape is dotted with shrines to the Golden Arches and an assortment of Pizza Temples, fasting seems out of place, out of step with the times. In fact, fasting has been in general disrepute both in and outside the church for many years. For example, in my research I could not find one single book published on the subject of fasting from 1861 to 1954, a period of nearly one hundred years. More recently there has developed a renewed interest in fasting, although it is often dogmatic and lacking in biblical balance.

What would account for this almost total disregard for a subject so frequently mentioned in Scripture and so ardently practiced by Christians through the centuries? Two things. First, fasting has developed a bad reputation as a result of the excessive ascetic practices of the Middle Ages. With the decline of the inward reality of the Christian faith, there developed an increasing tendency to stress the only thing left, the outward form. And whenever there is a form devoid of spiritual power, law will take over because law always carries with it a sense of manipulative power. Hence fasting was subjected to the most rigid regulations and practiced with extreme self-mortification and flagellation. Modern culture has reacted strongly to those excesses and has tended to confuse fasting with mortification.

There is a second reason why fasting has fallen on hard times in the past century. The constant propaganda fed us today has convinced us that if we do not have three large meals each day, with several snacks in between, we are on the verge of starvation. This, coupled with the

41

popular belief that it is a positive virtue to satisfy every human appetite, has made fasting seem obsolete. Anyone who seriously attempts
to fast is bombarded with objections. "I understand that fasting is in-
jurious to your health." "It will sap your strength so you can't
work." "Won't it destroy healthy body tissue?" All of this, of
course, is utter nonsense based upon prejudice. While the human body
can survive only a short time without air or water, it can go for many
days—usually about forty—before starvation begins. Without needing
to subscribe to the inflated claims of some groups, it is not an exagger-
ation to say that, when done correctly, fasting can have beneficial
physical effects.

Scripture has so much to say about fasting that we would do well to
look once again at this ancient Discipline. The list of biblical per-
sonages who fasted becomes a "Who's Who" of Scripture: Moses the
lawgiver, David the king, Elijah the Prophet, Esther the queen, Daniel
the seer, Anna the prophetess, Paul the apostle, Jesus Christ the incar-
nate Son. Many of the great Christians throughout church history
fasted and witnessed to its value; among them were Martin Luther,
John Calvin, John Knox, John Wesley, Jonathan Edwards, David
Brainerd, Charles Finney and Pastor Hsi of China.

Fasting, of course, is not an exclusively Christian Discipline; all the
major religions of the world recognize its merit. Zoroaster practiced
fasting as did Confucius and the Yogis of India. Plato, Socrates and
Aristotle all fasted. Even Hippocrates, the father of modern medicine,
believed in fasting. Now the fact that all these individuals, in and out
of Scripture, held fasting in high regard does not make it right or even
desirable, but it should give us enough pause to be willing to reevaluate the popular assumptions of our day concerning the Discipline
of Fasting.

Fasting in the Bible

Throughout Scripture fasting refers to abstaining from food for spiritual purposes. It stands in distinction to the hunger strike, the purpose
of which is to gain political power or attract attention for a good
cause. It is also distinct from health dieting, which stresses abstinence
from food, but for physical not spiritual purposes. Because of the
secularization of modern society, "fasting" (if it is done at all) is mo-

tivated either by vanity or the desire for power. That is not to say that these forms of "fasting" are necessarily wrong, but their objective is other than the fasting described in Scripture. Biblical fasting always centers on spiritual purposes.

In Scripture the normal means of fasting involved abstaining from all food, solid or liquid, but not from water. In the forty-day fast of Jesus, we are told that "he ate nothing" and toward the end of the fast that "he was hungry" and that Satan tempted Him to eat, indicating that the abstaining was from food but not from water (Lk. 4:2ff.). From a physical standpoint, this is what is usually involved in a fast.

Sometimes there is described what could be considered a partial fast; that is, there is a restriction of diet but not total abstention. Although the normal fast seemed to be the custom with the prophet Daniel, there was an occasion where for three weeks he "ate no delicacies, no meat or wine entered my mouth, nor did I anoint myself at all" (Dan. 10:3). We are not told the reason for this departure from his normal practice of fasting; perhaps his governmental tasks precluded it.

There are also several examples in Scripture of what has rightly been called an "absolute fast," or an abstaining from both food and water. It appears to be a desperate measure to meet a dire emergency. Upon learning that execution awaited herself and her people, Esther instructed Mordecai, "Go, gather all the Jews . . . and hold a fast on my behalf, and neither eat nor drink for three days, night or day. I and my maids will also fast as you do" (Esther 4:16). Paul engaged in a three-day absolute fast following his encounter with the living Christ (Acts 9:9). Since the human body cannot go without water much more than three days, both Moses and Elijah engaged in what must be considered supernatural absolute fasts of forty days (Deut. 9:9, 1 Kings 19:8). It must be underscored that the absolute fast is the exception and should never be engaged in unless one has a very clear command from God, and then for not more than three days.

In most cases fasting is a private matter between the individual and God. There are, however, occasional times of corporate or public fasts. The only annual public fast required in the Mosaic law was on the day of atonement (Lev. 23:27). It was to be *the day* in the Jewish calendar when the people were to be in sorrow and affliction as atonement for their sins. (Gradually other fast days were added until today there are over twenty!) Also, fasts were called in times of group or national emergency: "Blow the trumpet in Zion; sanctify a fast; call a solemn assembly; gather the people" (Joel 2:15). When Judah was invaded, King Jehoshaphat called the nation to fast (2 Chron. 20:1–4). In response to the preaching of Jonah, the entire city of Nineveh including the animals—involuntarily, no doubt—fasted. Before the trip back to Jerusalem, Ezra had the exiles fast and pray for safety on the bandit-infested road (Ezra 8:21–23).

The group fast can be a wonderful and powerful thing provided there is a prepared people who are of one mind in these matters. Churches or other groups who have serious problems could be substantially healed through unified group prayer and fasting. When a sufficient number of people rightly understand what is involved, national calls to prayer and fasting can also have beneficial results. In 1756 the king of Britain called for a day of solemn prayer and fasting because of a threatened invasion by the French. John Wesley recorded in his Journal on February 6:

> The fast day was a glorious day, such as London has scarce seen since the Restoration. Every church in the city was more than full, and a solemn seriousness sat on every face. Surely God heareth prayer, and there will yet be a lengthening of our tranquillity.

In a footnote he wrote, "Humility was turned into national rejoicing for the threatened invasion by the French was averted." [1]

Throughout history there has also developed what could be called regular fasts. By the time of Zechariah four regular fasts had developed (Zech. 8:19). The boast of the Pharisee in Jesus' parable evidently described a common practice of the day, "I fast twice a week" (Lk. 18:12).* The Didache urged two weekly fasts on Wednesdays and Fridays. Regular fasting was made obligatory at the Second Council of Orleans in the sixth century. John Wesley sought to revive the teaching of the Didache and urged early Methodists to fast on Wednesdays and Fridays. He felt so strongly about this matter, in fact, that he

---

* A frequent practice of the Pharisees was to fast on Mondays and Thursdays because those were market days and so there would be bigger audiences to see and admire their piety.

refused to ordain anyone to the Methodist ministry who did not fast on those two days.

Regular or weekly fasting has had such a profound effect in the lives of some that they have sought to find a biblical command for it, so that it may be urged upon all Christians. The search is in vain. There simply are no biblical laws that command regular fasting. Our freedom in the gospel, however, does not mean license; it means opportunity. Since there are no laws to bind us, we are free to fast on any day. Freedom for the apostle Paul meant that he was engaged in "fastings often" (2 Cor. 11:27, KJV). Always we should bear in mind the apostolic counsel, "Do not use your freedom as an opportunity for the flesh" (Gal. 5:13).

There is a "discipline" that has gained a certain popularity today which is akin, but not identical, to fasting. It is called "watchings," stemming from Paul's use of the term in connection with his sufferings for Christ (2 Cr. 6:5; 11:27, KJV). It refers to abstaining from sleep in order to attend to prayer or other spiritual duties. There is no indication that this has any central connection to fasting; otherwise we would be confined to very short fasts indeed! While "watchings" may have value and God at times may call us to do without sleep for specific needs, we must take care not to elevate into major obligations things that have only the slightest biblical precedent. Paul's warning should always be kept before us for, in any discussion of Disciplines, we will discover many things that ". . . have indeed an appearance of wisdom in promoting rigor of devotion and self-abasement and severity to the body, but they are of no value in checking the indulgence of the flesh" (Col. 2:23).

Is Fasting a Commandment?

One issue that understandably concerns many people is whether or not Scripture makes fasting obligatory upon all Christians. Numerous attempts have been made to answer that question, resulting in a variety of conclusions. One of the finest defenses of an affirmative answer was penned in 1580 by Thomas Cartwright in a book, something of a classic in the field, entitled *The Holy Exercise of a True Fast*.

Although many passages of Scripture deal with this subject, two stand out in importance. The first is Jesus' startling teaching about fasting in the Sermon on the Mount.* Two factors bear directly on the issue at hand. His teaching on fasting was directly in the context of His teaching on giving and praying. It is as if there is an almost unconscious assumption that giving, praying and fasting are all part of Christian devotion. We have no more reason to exclude fasting from the teaching than we do giving or praying. Second, Jesus stated, "When you fast . . ." (Mt. 6:16). He seemed to make the assumption that people would fast, and what was needed was instruction on how to do it properly. Martin Luther said, "It was not Christ's intention to reject or despise fasting . . . it was His intention to restore proper fasting." [2]

Having said this, however, we must go on to realize that those words of Jesus do not constitute a command. Jesus was giving instruction on the proper exercise of a common practice of His day. He did not speak a word about whether it was a right practice or if it should be continued. So although Jesus did not say "If you fast," neither did He say "You *must* fast."

The second crucial statement of Jesus about fasting came in response to a question by the disciples of John the Baptist. Perplexed over the fact that both they and the Pharisees fasted but Jesus' disciples did not, they asked "Why?" Jesus replied, "Can the wedding guests mourn as long as the bridegroom is with them? The days will come, when the bridegroom is taken away from them, and then they will fast" (Mt. 9:15). That is perhaps the most important statement in the New Testament on whether Christians should fast today.

In the coming of Jesus, a new day had dawned. The kingdom of God had come among them in present power. The Bridegroom was in their midst; it was a time for feasting, not fasting. There would, however, come a time for His disciples to fast, although not in the legalism of the old order.

The most natural interpretation of the days when Jesus' disciples will fast is the present church age, especially in light of its intricate connection with Jesus' statement on the new wineskins of the kingdom of God which follows immediately (Mt. 9:16–18). Arthur Wallis argues that Jesus is referring to the present church age, rather than just

---

* No attempt is made here to refute the heresy in Dispensationalism that the Sermon on the Mount applies to a future age rather than today. For a discussion of this issue see "The Hermeneutics of Dispensationalism" by Daniel P. Fuller (unpublished doctoral thesis at Northwestern Baptist Seminary, Chicago, Illinois).

the three-day period between His death and resurrection. He concludes his argument with these words:

> We are therefore compelled to refer the days of His absence to the period of this age, from the time He ascended to the Father until He shall return from heaven. This is evidently how His apostles understood Him, for it was not until after His ascension to the Father that we read of them fasting. (Acts 13:2,3) Before the Bridegroom left them He promised that He would come again to receive them to Himself. The Church still awaits the midnight cry, "Behold, the bridegroom! Come out to meet him." (Matt. 25:6) It is this age of the Church that is the period of the absent Bridegroom. It is this age of the Church to which our Master referred when He said, "Then they will fast." The time is now![3]

There is no way to escape the force of Jesus' words in that passage. He made it clear that He expected His disciples to fast after He was gone. Although the words are not couched in the form of a command, that is only a semantic technicality. It is clear from this passage that Christ both upheld the Discipline of fasting and that He anticipated that His followers would do it.

Perhaps it is best to avoid the term "command" since in the strictest sense Jesus did not command fasting. But it is obvious that He proceeded on the principle that the children of the kingdom of God would fast. For the person longing for a more intimate walk with God, these statements of Jesus are drawing words.

Where are the people today who will respond to the call of Christ? Have we become so accustomed to "cheap grace" that we instinctively shy away from more demanding calls to obedience? "Cheap grace is grace without discipleship, grace without the cross."[4] Why has the giving of money, for example, been unquestionably recognized as an element in Christian devotion and fasting so disputed? Certainly we have as much, if not more, evidence from the Bible for fasting as we have for giving. Perhaps in our affluent society fasting involves a far larger sacrifice than the giving of money.

The Purpose of Fasting

It is sobering to realize that the very first statement Jesus made about fasting dealt with the question of motive (Mt. 6:16–18). To use good things to our own ends is always the sign of false religion. How easy it is to take something like fasting and try to use it to get God to do what we want. At times there is such stress upon the blessings and benefits of fasting that we would be tempted to believe that with a little fast we could have the world, including God, eating out of our hand.

Fasting must forever center on God. It must be God-initiated and God-ordained. Like the prophetess Anna, we need to be "worshiping with fasting" (Lk. 2:37). Every other purpose must be subservient to God. like that apostolic band at Antioch, "fasting" and "worshiping the Lord" must be said in the same breath (Acts 13:2). C. H. Spurgeon wrote, "Our seasons of fasting and prayer at the Tabernacle have been high days indeed; never has Heaven's gate stood wider; never have our hearts been nearer the central Glory."[5]

God questioned the people in Zechariah's day, "When ye fasted . . . did ye at all fast unto me, even to me?" (Zech. 7:5, KJV). If our fasting is not unto God, we have failed. Physical benefits, success in prayer, the enduing with power, spiritual insights—these must never replace God as the center of our fasting. John Wesley declared, "First, let it [fasting] be done unto the Lord with our eye singly fixed on Him. Let our intention herein be this, and this alone, to glorify our Father which is in heaven. . . ."[6] That is the only way we will be saved from loving the blessing more than the Blesser.

Once the primary purpose is firmly fixed in our hearts, we are at liberty to understand that there are also secondary purposes in fasting. More than any other single Discipline, fasting reveals the things that control us. This is a wonderful benefit to the true disciple who longs to be transformed into the image of Jesus Christ. We cover up what is inside us with food and other good things, but in fasting these things surface. If pride controls us, it will be revealed almost immediately. David said, "I humbled my soul with fasting" (Ps. 69:10). Anger, bitterness, jealousy, strife, fear—if they are within us, they will surface during fasting. At first we will rationalize that our anger is due to our hunger; then we know that we are angry because the spirit of anger is within us. We can rejoice in this knowledge because we know that healing is available through the power of Christ.*

Fasting helps us keep our balance in life. How easily we begin to

---

*This will be elaborated upon in future chapters.

allow nonessentials to take precedence in our lives. How quickly we crave things we do not need until we are enslaved by them. Paul wrote, " 'All things are lawful for me,' but I will not be enslaved by anything" (1 Cor. 6:12). Our human cravings and desires are like a river that tends to overflow its banks; fasting helps keep them in their proper channel. "I pommel my body and subdue it," said Paul (1 Cor. 9:27). Likewise, David wrote, "I afflicted myself with fasting" (Ps. 35:13). That is no asceticism: it is discipline and discipline brings freedom. In the fourth century Asterius said that fasting insured that the stomach would not make the body boil like a kettle to the hindering of the soul.[7]

Numerous people have written on the many other values of fasting such as increased effectiveness in intercessory prayer, guidance in decisions, increased concentration, deliverance for those in bondage, physical well-being, revelations, etc. In this, as in all matters, we can expect God to reward those who diligently seek Him.

The Practice of Fasting

Modern men and women are largely ignorant of the practical aspects of fasting. Those who desire to fast need to acquaint themselves with this information.

As with all the Disciplines, a progression should be observed; it is wise to learn to walk well before we try to run. Begin with a partial fast of twenty-four hours' duration; many have found lunch to lunch to be the best time. This would mean that you would not eat two meals. Fresh fruit juices are excellent. Attempt this once a week for several weeks. In the beginning you will be fascinated with the physical aspects, but the most important thing to monitor is the inner attitude of worship. Outwardly you will be performing the regular duties of your day, but inwardly you will be in prayer and adoration, song and worship. In a new way, cause every task of the day to be a sacred ministry to the Lord. However mundane your duties, they are for you a sacrament. Cultivate a "gentle receptiveness to divine breathings."[8] Break your fast with a light meal of fresh fruits and vegetables and a good deal of inner rejoicing.

After two or three weeks, you are prepared to attempt a twenty-four-hour normal fast. Use only water but use healthy amounts of it.

Many feel distilled water is best. If the taste of the water bothers you, add one teaspoon of lemon juice. You will probably feel some hunger pains or discomfort before the time is up. That is not real hunger; your stomach has been trained through years of conditioning to give signals of hunger at certain hours. In many ways your stomach is like a spoiled child, and spoiled children do not need indulgence, they need discipline. Martin Luther said ". . . the flesh was wont to grumble dreadfully." [9] You must not give in to this grumbling." Ignore the signals or even tell your "spoiled child" to calm down and in a brief time the hunger pains will pass. If not, sip another glass of water and the stomach will be satisfied. You are to be the master of your stomach, not its slave. If family obligations permit it, devote the time you would normally eat to meditation and prayer.

It should go without saying that you should follow Jesus' counsel to refrain from calling attention to what you are doing. The only ones who should know you are fasting are those who have to know. If you call attention to your fasting, people will be impressed and, as Jesus said, that will be your reward. You, however, are fasting for far greater and deeper rewards. The following was written by an individual who, as an experiment, had committed himself to fast once a week for two years. Notice the progression from the superficial aspects of fasting toward the deeper rewards.

1. I felt it a great accomplishment to go a whole day without food. Congratulated myself on the fact that I found it so easy. . . .

2. Began to see that the above was hardly the goal of fasting. Was helped in this by beginning to feel hunger. . . .

3. Began to relate the food fast to other areas of my life where I was more compulsive. . . . I did not have to have a seat on the bus to be contented, or to be cool in the summer and warm when it was cold.

4. . . . Reflected more on Christ's suffering and the suffering of those who are hungry and have hungry babies. . . .

5. Six months after beginning the fast discipline, I began to see why a two-year period has been suggested. The experience changes along the way. Hunger on fast days became acute, and the temptation to eat stronger. For the first time I was using the

day to find God's will for my life. Began to think about what it meant to *surrender* one's life.

6. I now know that prayer and fasting must be intricately bound together. There is no other way, and yet that way is not yet combined in me.[10]

Having achieved several fasts with a degree of spiritual success, move on to a thirty-six-hour fast: three meals. With that accomplished, it is time to seek the Lord as to whether He wants you to go on a longer fast. Three to seven days is a good time period and will probably have a substantial impact on the course of your life.

It is well to know the process your body goes through in the course of a longer fast. The first three days are usually the most difficult in terms of physical discomfort and hunger pains. The body is beginning to rid itself of the toxic poisons that have built up over years of poor eating habits, and it is not a comfortable process. This is the reason for the coating on the tongue and bad breath. Do not be disturbed by these symptoms; rather be grateful for the increased health and well-being that will result. You may experience headaches during this time, especially if you are an avid coffee or tea drinker. Those are mild withdrawal symptoms which will pass, though they may be very unpleasant for a time.

By the fourth day the hunger pains are beginning to subside though you will have feelings of weakness and occasional dizziness. The dizziness is only temporary and caused by sudden changes in position. Move more slowly and you will have no difficulty. The weakness can come to the point where the simplest task takes great effort. Rest is the best remedy. Many find this the most difficult period of the fast.

By the sixth or seventh day you will begin to feel stronger and more alert. Hunger pains will continue to diminish until by the ninth or tenth day they are only a minor irritation. The body will have eliminated the bulk of toxic poisons and you will feel good. Your sense of concentration will be sharpened and you will feel as if you could continue fasting indefinitely. Physically this is the most enjoyable part of the fast.

Anywhere from twenty-one to forty days or longer, depending upon the individual, hunger pains will return. This is the first stage of starvation and signals that the body has used up all its excess reserves and is beginning to draw on the living tissue. The fast should be broken at this time.

The amount of weight lost during a fast varies greatly with the individual. In the beginning the loss of two pounds a day, decreasing to one pound per day as the fast progresses, is normal. During fasting you will feel the cold more, simply because the body metabolism is not producing the usual amount of heat. If care is observed to keep warm, this is no difficulty.

It should be obvious to all that there are some people who for physical reasons should not fast. Diabetics, expectant mothers, and heart patients should not fast. If you have any question about your fitness to fast, seek medical advice.

Before commencing an extended fast, some are tempted to eat a good deal to "stock up." That is most unwise; in fact, slightly lighter than normal meals are best for the day or two before a fast. You would also be well advised to abstain from coffee or tea three days before beginning a longer fast. If the last meal in the stomach is fresh fruits and vegetables, you should have no difficulty with constipation.

An extended fast should be broken with fruits or vegetable juice. Small amounts should be taken at first. Remember that the stomach has shrunk considerably and the entire digestive system has gone into a kind of hibernation. By the second day you should be able to eat fruit and then milk or yogurt. Next you can take fresh salads and cooked vegetables. Avoid all salad dressing, grease or starch. Extreme care should be taken not to overeat. It is a good thing during this time to consider future diet and eating habits to see if you need to be more disciplined and in control of your appetite.

Although the physical aspects of fasting intrigue us, we must never forget that the major work of scriptural fasting is in the realm of the spirit. What goes on spiritually is of much more consequence than what is happening bodily. You will be engaged in spiritual warfare that will necessitate all the weapons of Ephesians six. One of the most spiritually critical periods is at the close of the physical fast when we have a natural tendency to relax. But I do not want to leave the impression that all fasting is a heavy spiritual struggle—I have not found it so. It is also ". . . righteousness and peace and joy in the Holy Spirit" (Rom. 14:17).

Fasting can bring breakthroughs in the spiritual realm that could never be had in any other way. It is a means of God's grace and blessing that should not be neglected any longer. Wesley declared:

> . . . it was not merely by the light of reason . . . that the people of God have been, in all ages, directed to use fasting as a means: . . . but they have been . . . taught it of God Himself, by clear and open revelations of His Will. . . . Now, whatever reasons there were to quicken those of old, in the zealous and constant discharge of this duty, they are of equal force still to quicken us.[11]

Now is the time for all who hear the voice of Christ to obey it.

5. THE DISCIPLINE OF STUDY

He that studies only men, will get the body of knowledge without the soul; and he that studies only books, the soul without the body. He that to what he sees, adds observation, and to what he reads, reflection, is in the right road to knowledge, provided that in scrutinizing the hearts of others, he neglects not his own.—Caleb Colton

The purpose of the Spiritual Disciplines is the total transformation of the person. It aims at replacing old destructive habits of thought with new life-giving habits. Nowhere is this purpose more clearly seen than in the Discipline of study. The apostle Paul tells us that the way we are transformed is through the renewal of the mind (Rom. 12:2). The mind is renewed by applying it to those things that will transform it. "Finally, brethren, whatever is true, whatever is honorable, whatever is just, whatever is pure, whatever is lovely, whatever is gracious, if there is anything worthy of praise, *think* about these things" (Phil. 4:8). The Discipline of study is the primary vehicle to bring us to "*think* about these things." Therefore, we should rejoice that we are not left to our own devices but have been given this means of God's grace for the changing of our inner spirit.

Many Christians remain in bondage to fears and anxieties simply because they do not avail themselves of the Discipline of study. They may be faithful in church attendance and earnest in fulfilling their religious duties and still they are not changed. I am not here speaking only of those who are going through mere religious forms, but of those who are genuinely seeking to worship and obey Jesus Christ as Lord and Master. They may sing with gusto, pray in the Spirit, live as obediently as they know, even receive divine visions and revelations; and yet the tenor of their lives remains unchanged. Why? Because they have never taken up one of the central ways God uses to change us: study. Jesus made it unmistakably clear that it is the knowledge of the truth that will set us free. "You will know the truth and the truth will make you free" (Jn. 8:32). Good feelings will not free us. Ecstatic experiences will not free us. Getting "high on Jesus" will not free us. Without a knowledge of the truth, we will not be free.

This principle is true in every area of human endeavor. It is true in biology and mathematics. It is true in marriages and other human relationships. But it is especially true in reference to the spiritual life. Many are hampered and confused in the spiritual walk by simple ignorance of the truth. Worse yet, many have been brought into the most cruel bondage by false teaching. "You traverse sea and land to make a single proselyte, and when he becomes a proselyte, you make him twice as much a child of hell as yourselves" (Mt. 23:15).

Let us therefore apply ourselves to learning what constitutes the Spiritual Discipline of study, to identify its pitfalls, to practice it with joy, and to experience the liberation it brings.

What Is Study?

Study is a specific kind of experience in which through careful observation of objective structures we cause thought processes to move in a certain way. Perhaps we study a tree or book. We see it, feel it. As we do, *our thought processes take on an order conforming to the order in the tree or book.* When done with concentration, perception and repetition, ingrained habits of thought are formed.

The Old Testament instructs that the laws be written on gates and doorposts, and bound to the wrists so that "they shall be as frontlets between your eyes" (Deut. 11:18). The purpose of that instruction was to direct the mind repeatedly and regularly in certain modes of thought about God and human relations. A rosary or a prayer wheel has the same objective in mind. Of course, the New Testament replaces laws written on the doorposts with laws written on the heart and leads us to Jesus, our ever-present and inward Teacher.

We must once again emphasize that the ingrained habits of thought that are formed *will* conform to the order of the thing being studied. *What* we study determines what kind of habits are to be formed. That is why Paul urged us to center on things that are true, honorable, just, pure, lovely and gracious.

The process that occurs in study should be distinguished from meditation. Meditation is devotional; study is analytical. Meditation will relish a word; study will explicate it.

Although meditation and study often overlap and function concurrently, they constitute two distinct experiences. Study provides a certain objective framework within which meditation can successfully function.

In study there are two "books" to be studied: verbal and nonverbal. Books and lectures, therefore, constitute only half of the field of study, perhaps less. The world of nature and, most important, the careful observation of events and actions are the primary nonverbal fields of study.

The principal task of study is a perception into the reality of a given situation, encounter, book, etc. One person could go through, for example, the Watergate scandal without any perception whatever of the real nature of that tragic situation. But if a person would carefully observe and reflect upon what was occurring he or she would learn a great deal.

Four Steps

Study involves four steps. The first is repetition. Repetition is a way of regularly channeling the mind in a specific direction, thus ingraining habits of thought. Repetition has received something of a bad name today. It is important, however, to realize that sheer repetition without even understanding what is being repeated does affect the inner mind. Ingrained habits of thought can be formed by repetition alone, thus changing behavior. That is the central rationale behind psychocybernetics which trains the individual to repeat certain affirmations regularly (e.g., I love myself unconditionally). It is not even important that the person believe what he or she is repeating, only that it be repeated. The inner mind is thus trained and will eventually respond by modifying behavior to conform to the affirmation. This principle has, of course, been known for centuries but only recently has it received scientific confirmation.

That is why the issue of television programming is so important. With innumerable murders committed each evening on prime time

TV, the repetition alone will train the inner mind in destructive thought patterns.*

Concentration is the second step in study. If in addition to bringing the mind repeatedly to the subject matter the person will concentrate on what is being studied, learning is vastly increased. Concentration centers the mind. It focuses the attention on the thing being studied. The human mind has incredible ability to concentrate. It is constantly receiving thousands of stimuli, every one of which it is able to store in its memory banks while focusing on only a few. This natural ability of the brain is enhanced when with singleness of purpose we center our attention upon a desired object of study.

When we not only repeatedly channel the mind in a particular direction, centering our attention on the subject, but understand what we are studying, we reach a new level. Comprehension then is the third step in the Discipline of study. Comprehension leads to insight and discernment. It provides the basis for a true perception of reality.

One further step is needed: reflection. Although comprehension defines what we are studying, reflection defines the *significance* of what we are studying. To reflect, to ruminate, on the events of our time will lead us to the inner reality of those events. Reflection brings us to see things from God's perspective. In reflection we come to understand not only our subject matter but ourselves. Jesus spoke often of ears that do not hear and eyes that do not see. When we ponder the meaning of what we study, we come to hear and see things in a new way.

It soon becomes obvious that study demands humility. It cannot happen until we are willing to be subject to the subject matter. We must submit to the system. We must come as student, not teacher. Not only is study directly dependent upon humility, but it is conducive to it. Arrogance and a teachable spirit are mutually exclusive.

All of us know individuals who have taken some course of study or attained some academic degree who parade their information in an offensive manner. We should feel profound sorrow for such people. They do not understand the Spiritual Discipline of study. They have mistaken the accumulation of information for knowledge. They

* At the time of this writing there is a case in the courts in which the defense is claiming that the cause of a teen-ager killing his grandfather was his watching crime on television.

equate the spouting of words with wisdom. How tragic! The apostle John defined eternal life as the knowledge of God. ''And this is eternal life, that they know thee the only true God, and Jesus Christ whom thou hast sent'' (Jn. 17:3). Even a touch of this experiential knowledge is sufficient to give us a profound sense of humility.

Now, having laid the basis, let us move on to consider the practical implementation of the Discipline of study.

Study of Books

When we consider study we most naturally think of books or other writings. Though only half the field, as I stated earlier, and the most obvious, they are clearly important.

Unfortunately, many seem to think that studying a book is a simple task. No doubt that flippant attitude accounts for the poor reading habits of so many people. The studying of a book is an extremely complex matter, especially to the novice. Like tennis or typing, when you are first learning it seems that there are a thousand details to be mastered and you wonder how on earth it is possible to keep everything in mind at the same time. Once you are proficient, however, the mechanics become second nature and you can concentrate on the game of tennis or the material to be typed.

The same is true with studying a book. Study is an exacting art involving a labyrinth of details. The major obstacle is convincing people that they must *learn* to study. Most people assume that because they know how to read words they know how to study. This limited grasp of the nature of study explains why so many people gain so little from reading books.

Three intrinsic and three extrinsic rules govern the successful study of a book.*

The intrinsic rules may in the beginning necessitate three separate readings but in time can be done concurrently. The first reading involves *understanding* the book: what is the author saying? The second reading involves *interpreting* the book: what does the author mean? The third reading involves *evaluating* the book: is the author right or

---

* These matters are covered in great detail in Mortimer J. Adler's *How to Read a Book* (New York: Simon and Schuster, 1940). I am indebted to him for these insights into the Discipline of study.

wrong? Most of us tend to do the third reading first and often never do the first and second readings at all. We give a critical analysis of a book before we understand what it says. We judge a book to be right or wrong before we interpret its meaning. The wise writer of Ecclesiastes said that there is a time for every matter under heaven, and the time for critical analysis of a book comes *after* careful understanding and interpretation.

The intrinsic rules of study, however, are in themselves inadequate. To read successfully we need the extrinsic aids of experience, other books and live discussion.

Experience is the only way we can interpret and relate to what we read. Experience that has been understood and reflected upon informs and enlightens our study.

Other books can include dictionaries, commentaries and other interpretative literature, but more significant are other great books that precede or further the issue being studied. Books often have meaning only when they are read in relation to other books. People will find it nearly impossible to understand Romans or Hebrews, for example, without a grounding in the literature of the Old Testament. It is really impossible to read *The Federalist Papers* with understanding without first having read the Articles of Confederation and the U.S. Constitution. The great books which take up the central issues of life interact with each other. They cannot be read in isolation.

Live discussion refers to the ordinary interaction that occurs among human beings as they pursue a particular course of study. We interact with the author, we interact with each other—and new creative ideas are born.

The first and most important book we are to study is the Bible. The psalmist asked, "How can a young man keep his way pure?" He then answered his own question, "By guarding it according to thy word," and added, "I have laid up thy word in my heart, that I might not sin against thee" (Ps. 119:9, 11). Probably the "word" which the psalmist is referring to is the Torah, but Christians throughout the centuries have found this to be true in their study throughout Scripture. "All scripture is inspired by God and profitable for teaching, for reproof, for correction, and for training in righteousness, that the man of God may be complete, equipped for every good work" (2 Tim. 3:16, 17). Note that the central purpose is not doctrinal purity (though that is no doubt involved) but inner transformation. When we come to the Scripture we come to be changed, not to amass information.

We must understand, however, that a vast difference exists between the study of Scripture and the devotional reading of Scripture. In the study of Scripture a high priority is placed upon interpretation: what it means. In the devotional reading of Scripture a high priority is placed upon application: what it means for me. In study we are not seeking spiritual ecstasy; in fact, ecstasy can be a hindrance. When we study a book of the Bible we are seeking to be controlled by the intent of the author. We are determined to hear what he is saying, not what we would like him to say. We are willing to pay the price of barren day after barren day until the meaning is clear. This process revolutionizes our life.

The apostle Peter found some things in the epistles of "our beloved brother Paul" that were "hard to understand" (2 Peter 3:15, 16). If Peter found it so, we will as well. We will need to work at it. Daily devotional reading is certainly commendable but it is not study. Anyone who is after "a little word from God for today" is not interested in the Discipline of study.

The average adult Sunday School is far too superficial and devotional to help us study the Bible, although some churches believe sufficiently in study to offer serious courses in the Bible. Perhaps you live in proximity to a seminary or university where you can audit courses. If so, you are fortunate, especially if you find a teacher who is dispensing *life* as well as information. If, however, that is not the case (and even if it is) you can do several things to begin studying the Bible.

Some of my most profitable experiences of study have come through structuring a private retreat for myself. Usually it involves two to three days. No doubt you will object that given your schedule you could not possibly find that kind of time. I want you to know that it is no easier for me to secure that time than for anyone else. I fight and struggle for every retreat, scheduling it into my datebook many weeks in advance. I have suggested this idea to groups and found that professional people with busy schedules, laborers with rigid schedules, housewives with large families, and others can, in fact, find time for a private study retreat. I have discovered that the most difficult problem is not finding time but convincing myself that this is important enough to find the time.

Scripture tells us that following the marvelous resurrection of Dorcas, Peter "tarried many days in Joppa with one Simon a tanner" (Acts 9:43, KJV). It was while tarrying in Joppa that the Holy Spirit got through to Peter (with visual aids no less) about his racism. What would have happened if, instead of tarrying, Peter had immediately struck out on a speaking tour to tell of the resurrection of Dorcas? Is it possible that he would have failed to come to that shattering insight from the Holy Spirit, "Truly I perceive that God shows no partiality, but in every nation any one who fears him and does what is right is acceptable to him" (Acts 10:34)? No one knows. But I do know this: God desires for all of us various "tarrying" places where He can teach us in a special way.

For many people, a weekend is a good time for such an experience. Others can arrange a block of time in the middle of the week. If only one day is possible, often a Sunday is excellent.

The best place is anywhere as long as it is away from home. To leave the house not only sets you free from the telephone and domestic responsibilities but it also sets your mind into a learning mode. Motels work well, as do cabins. Camping is less desirable since you are more distracted by the tasks of living. Often Catholic retreat centers are receptive and can accommodate private retreatants.

Organized group retreats almost never take study seriously, so you will most certainly need to structure the retreat yourself. Because you are alone you will need to discipline yourself and your time carefully. If you are new at it you will not want to overdo and thus burn yourself out. With experience, however, you will hope to put in ten to twelve hours of good study each day.

What should you study? That depends on what you need. I do not know your needs but I know that one of the great needs among Christians today is simply the reading of large portions of Scripture. So much of our Bible reading is fragmented and sporadic. I have actually known students who have taken courses in the Bible and never even read as a whole the book of the Bible being studied. Consider taking a major book of the Bible like Genesis or Jeremiah and read it straight through. Notice the structure and flow of the book. Note areas of difficulty and return to them later. Jot down thoughts and impressions. Sometimes it is wise to combine the study of the Bible with the study of some great devotional classic. Such retreat experiences can transform your life.

Another approach to the study of the Bible is to take a smaller book, like Ephesians or 1 John, and read it through each day for a month. More than any single effort this will put the structure of the book into your mind. Read it without trying to fit it into established categories. Expect to hear new things in new ways. Keep a journal of your findings. In the course of these studies you will obviously want to make use of the best secondary aids available.

In addition to studying the Bible, do not neglect the study of some of the experiential classics in Christian literature. Begin with *The Confessions of St. Augustine*. Next turn to *The Imitation of Christ* by Thomas à Kempis. Don't neglect *The Practice of the Presence of God* by Brother Lawrence. For an added pleasure read *The Little Flowers of St. Francis* by Brother Ugolino. Perhaps you might want something a bit heavier next like the *Pensées* of Blaise Pascal. Enjoy the *Table Talks* of Martin Luther before you wade into Calvin's *Institutes of the Christian Religion*. Consider reading the pacemaker of religious journal writing, *The Journal of George Fox*, or perhaps the better-known *Journal of John Wesley*. Read carefully William Law's *A Serious Call to a Devout and Holy Life* (its words carry a contemporary ring). From the twentieth century read *A Testament of Devotion* by Thomas Kelly, *The Cost of Discipleship* by Dietrich Bonhoeffer and *Mere Christianity* by C. S. Lewis.

Obviously that is only a sampling. I completely passed over the *Revelations of Divine Love* by Juliana of Norwich, *Introduction to the Devout Life* by Francis de Sales, *The Journal of John Woolman,* and many other books. Nor should we forget the great body of literature by men and women from many disciplines. Many of these thinkers have unusual perception into the human predicament. Eastern writers like Lao-tse of China and Zarathustra of Persia, Shakespeare and Milton, Cervantes and Dante, Tolstoy and Dostoevski, and in our century, Dag Hammarskjöld.

One word of caution is in order. Do not be overwhelmed or discouraged by all the books you have not read. You will probably not read all of those listed here and will undoubtedly read others not noted.

These have been listed to encourage you by demonstrating the excellent amount of literature at our disposal to guide us in the spiritual walk. Many others have traveled the same path and have left markers. Remember that the key to the Discipline of study is not reading many books but experiencing what we do read.

Study of Nonverbal "Books"

We now come to the least recognized but perhaps the most important field of study: the observation of reality in things, events and actions. The easiest place to begin is with nature. It is not difficult to see that the created order has something to teach us.

Isaiah tells us that ". . . the mountains and the hills before you shall break forth into singing, and all the trees of the field shall clap their hands" (Is. 55:12). The handiwork of the Creator can speak to us and teach us if we will listen. Martin Buber told the story of the rabbi who went to a pond every day at dawn to learn "the song with which the frogs praise God." [1]

We begin the study of nature by paying attention. We *see* flowers or birds. We observe them carefully and prayerfully. André Gide described the time when during a classroom lecture he observed a moth being reborn from its chrysalis. He was filled with wonder, awe, joy at this metamorphosis, this resurrection. Enthusiastically he showed it to his professor who replied with a note of disapproval, "What! Didn't you know that a chrysalis is the envelope of a butterfly? Every butterfly you see has come out of a chrysalis. It's perfectly natural." Disillusioned, Gide wrote, "Yes, indeed, I knew my *natural* history as well, perhaps better than he. . . . But because it was natural, could he not see that it was marvelous? Poor creature! From that day, I took a dislike to him and a loathing to his lessons." [2] Who wouldn't! Gide's professor had only amassed information, he had not studied. And so the first step in the study of nature is reverent observation. A leaf can speak of order and variety, complexity and symmetry. Evelyn Underhill wrote:

> Gather yourself up, as the exercises of recollection have taught you to do. Then—with attention no longer frittered amongst the petty accidents and interests of your personal life, but poised,

tense, ready for the work you shall demand of it—stretch out by a distinct act of loving will towards one of the myriad manifestations of life that surround you: and which, in an ordinary way, you hardly notice unless you happen to need them. Pour yourself out towards it, do not draw its image towards you. Deliberate—more, impassioned—attentiveness, an attentiveness which soon transcends all consciousness of yourself, as separate from and attending to the thing seen; this is the condition of success. As to the object of contemplation, it matters little. From Alp to insect, anything will do, provided that your attitude be right: for all things in this world towards which you are stretching out are linked together, and one truly apprehended will be the gateway to the rest.[3]

The next step is to make friends with the flowers and trees and little creatures that creep upon the earth. Like the fabled Dr. Doolittle, talk with the animals. Of course you can't really talk to each other . . . or can you? There is certainly a communication that goes beyond words—and animals, even plants, seem to respond to our friendship and compassion. I know this because I have experimented with it, and so have some first-rate scientists, and we have found it to be true. Perhaps the stories about St. Francis of Assisi taming the wolf of Gubbio and preaching to the birds is not so farfetched. Of this much we can be sure: if we love the creation we will learn from it. In *The Brothers Karamazov* Dostoevski counseled:

Love all God's creation, the whole and every grain of sand in it. Love every leaf, every ray of God's light. Love the animals, love the plants, love everything. If you love everything, you will perceive the divine mystery in things. Once you perceive it, you will begin to comprehend it better every day.[4]

There are, of course, many other "books" beside nature that we should study. If you will observe the relationships that go on between human beings you will receive a graduate-level education. Watch, for example, how much of our speech is aimed at justifying our actions. We find it almost impossible to act and allow the act to speak for itself. No, we must explain it, justify it, demonstrate the rightness of it. Why is it we feel this compulsion to set the record straight? Because of pride and fear. Our reputation is at stake!

That trait is particularly easy to observe among salespeople, writers, ministers, professors—all those who earn their living by being good with words. If, however, we will make ourselves one of the principal subjects of study we will be gradually delivered from arrogance. We will be unable to pray like the Pharisee, "God, I thank thee that I am not like other men . . ." (Lk. 18:11).

Become attentive to the ordinary relationships you encounter throughout your day: at home, work, school. Notice the things that control people. Remember, you are not trying to condemn or judge anyone, you are only trying to learn. If you do find a judging spirit emerging within you, observe that and learn.

As I mentioned earlier, one of the principal objects of our study should be ourselves. We should learn the things that control *us*. Observe your inner feelings and mood swings. What controls your moods? What can you learn about yourself from that?*

In doing all this we are not trying to become amateur psychologists or sociologists. Nor are we obsessed with excessive introspection. We study these matters with a spirit of humility and needing a large dose of grace. We are wanting only to follow the dictum of Socrates: "Know thyself." And through the blessed Holy Spirit we are expecting Jesus to be our living and ever-present Teacher.

We would do well to study institutions and cultures and the forces that shape them. Also, we should ponder the events of our time—noting first, with a spirit of discernment, what our culture thinks is or is not a "great event." Look at the value systems of a culture—not what people say they are, but what they actually are. And one of the clearest ways to see the values of American culture is to observe television commercials.

Ask questions. What are the assets and liabilities of a technological society? What has the fast-food industry done to the tradition of a family gathering for dinner? Why do we find it difficult in our culture to have time to develop relationships? Is Western individualism valuable or destructive? What in our culture is in line with the gospel and what

---

*This counsel is for reasonably mature and well-adjusted individuals. It is *not* for mental depressives or others who are bowed low by the burdens of life. For them these exercises are too depressing and self-defeating. If you find your days too heavy for this kind of study, please do not attempt it. But there is hope, and there is something you can do. See the chapters on Confession and Guidance.

is at odds with it? One of the most important functions of Christian prophets in our day is the ability to perceive the consequences of various inventions and other forces in our culture and to make value judgments upon them.

Study produces joy. Like any novice we will find it hard work in the beginning. But the greater our proficiency the greater our joy. Alexander Pope said, "There is no study that is not capable of delighting us after a little application to it."[5] Study is well worth our most serious effort.

PART II

The Outward
Disciplines

6. THE DISCIPLINE OF SIMPLICITY

*When we are truly in this interior simplicity our whole ap-
pearance is franker, more natural. This true simplicity
. . . makes us conscious of a certain openness, gentleness, innocence, gaiety, and serenity, which is charming
when we see it near to and continually, with pure eyes. O,
how amiable this simplicity is! Who will give it to me? I
leave all for this. It is the pearl of the Gospel.*
—François Fénelon

Simplicity is freedom. Duplicity is bondage. Simplicity brings joy and
balance. Duplicity brings anxiety and fear. The preacher of Ecclesiastes observed that "God made man simple; man's complex problems
are of his own devising" (Eccles. 7:39, Jerusalem Bible). Because
many of us are experiencing the liberation God brings through simplicity we are once again singing an old Shaker hymn:

> It's a gift to be simple,
> It's a gift to be free,
> It's a gift to come down where we ought to be,
> And when we see ourselves in a way that's right,
> We will live in a valley of love and delight!
>
> When true simplicity is gained,
> To live and to love we will not be ashamed,
> To turn and to turn will be our delight,
> Till by turning, turning
> We turn 'round right.

The Christian Discipline of simplicity is an *inward* reality that results in an *outward* life-style. Both the inward and outward aspects of
simplicity are essential. We deceive ourselves if we believe we can
possess the inward reality without its having a profound effect on how

we live. To attempt to arrange an outward life-style of simplicity without the inward reality leads to deadly legalism.

Simplicity begins in inward focus and unity. It means to live out of what Thomas Kelly called "The Divine Center." Kierkegaard captured the nucleus of Christian simplicity in the profound title of his book, *Purity of Heart Is to Will One Thing*.

Experiencing the inward reality liberates us outwardly. Speech becomes truthful and honest. The lust for status and position is gone, because we no longer need status and position. We cease from showy extravagance, not on the grounds of being unable to afford it, but on the grounds of principle. Our goods become available to others. We join the experience that Richard E. Byrd recorded in his journal after months alone in the barren Arctic: "I am learning . . . that a man can live profoundly without masses of things."[1]

Contemporary culture lacks both the inward reality and the outward life-style of simplicity.

Inwardly modern man is fractured and fragmented. He is trapped in a maze of competing attachments. One moment he makes decisions on the basis of sound reason and the next moment out of fear of what others will think of him. He has no unity or focus around which life is oriented.

Because we lack a divine Center our need for security has led us into an insane attachment to things. We must clearly understand that the lust for affluence in contemporary society is psychotic. It is psychotic because it has completely lost touch with reality. We crave things we neither need nor enjoy. "We buy things we do not want to impress people we do not like."[2] Where planned obsolescence leaves off, psychological obsolescence takes over. We are made to feel ashamed to wear clothes or drive cars until they are worn out. The mass media have convinced us that to be out of step with fashion is to be out of step with reality. It is time we awaken to the fact that conformity to a sick society is to be sick. Until we see how unbalanced our culture has become at this point we will not be able to deal with the mammon spirit within ourselves nor will we desire Christian simplicity.

This psychosis permeates even our mythology. The modern hero is the poor boy who becomes rich rather than the Franciscan or Buddhist ideal of the rich boy who voluntarily becomes poor. (We still find it hard to imagine that either could happen to a girl!) Covetousness we call ambition. Hoarding we call prudence. Greed we call industry.

Further, it is important to understand that the modern counter culture is hardly an improvement. It is a superficial change in life-style without seriously dealing with the root problems of a consumer society. Because the counter culture has always lacked a positive center it has inevitably degenerated into trivia. Art Gish has said:

> Much of the counter culture is a mirror of the worst features of the old sick society. The revolution is not free dope, free sex, and abortions on demand. That is the dying gasps of an old culture and will not lead to new life. The pseudo-libertarian eroticism, elements of sado-masochism, and sexist advertisements in much of the underground press is part of the perversion of the old order and an expression of death. Many in the underground are living the same values of the establishment, only in inverted form.[3]

Courageously we need to articulate new, more human ways to live. We should take exception to the modern psychosis that defines people by how much they can produce or what they earn. We should experiment with bold new alternatives to the present death-giving system. The Spiritual Discipline of simplicity is not a lost dream but a recurrent vision throughout history. It can be recaptured today. It must be.

The Bible and Simplicity

Before attempting to forge a Christian view of simplicity it is necessary to destroy the prevailing notion that the Bible is ambiguous about economic issues. So often it is felt that our response to wealth is an individual matter. The Bible's teaching in this area is said to be strictly a matter of private interpretation. We try to believe that Jesus did not address himself to practical economic questions.

No serious reading of Scripture can substantiate such a view. The biblical injunctions against the exploitation of the poor and the accumulation of wealth are clear and straightforward. The Bible challenges nearly every economic value of contemporary society. For example, the Old Testament takes exception to the popular notion of an absolute right to private property. The earth belonged to God and therefore could not be held perpetually, and on the year of Jubilee all land reverted to its original owner. In fact, the purpose of the year of Jubilee was to provide a regular redistribution of wealth, since wealth itself was viewed as belonging to God and not man. Such a radical view of economics flies in the face of nearly all modern belief and practice. Had Israel faithfully observed the Jubilee it would have dealt a death blow to the perennial problem of the rich becoming richer and the poor becoming poorer.

Constantly the Bible deals decisively with the inner spirit of slavery that an idolatrous attachment to wealth brings. "If riches increase, set not your heart on them," counsels the psalmist (Ps. 62:10). The tenth commandment is against covetousness, the inner lust to "have," which leads to stealing and oppression. The wise sage understood that "he who trusts in his riches will wither" (Prov. 11:28).

Jesus declared war on the materialism of His day. The Aramaic term for wealth was "mammon" and Jesus condemned it as a rival God: "No servant can serve two masters; for either he will hate the one and love the other, or he will be devoted to the one and despise the other. You cannot serve God and mammon" (Lk. 16:13). He spoke frequently and unambiguously to economic issues. He said, "Blessed are you poor, for yours is the kingdom of God" and "Woe to you that are rich, for you have received your consolation" (Lk. 6:20, 24). He graphically depicted the difficulty of the wealthy entering the kingdom of God to be like a camel walking through the eye of a needle. With God, of course, all things are possible, but Jesus clearly understood the difficulty. He saw the grip that wealth can have on a person. He knew that "where your treasure is, there will your heart be also," which is precisely why He commanded His followers: "Do not lay up for yourselves treasures on earth" (Mt. 6:21, 19). He was not saying that the heart should or should not be where the treasure is. He was stating the plain fact that wherever you find the treasure you *will* find the heart.

He exhorted the rich young ruler not just to have an inner attitude of detachment from his possessions but literally to get rid of his possessions if he wanted the kingdom of God (Mt. 19:16–22). He said, "Take heed, and beware of all covetousness; for a man's life does not consist in the abundance of his possessions" (Lk. 12:15). He counseled people who came seeking God, "Sell your possessions, and give alms; provide yourselves with purses that do not grow old, with a treasure in the heavens that does not fail . . ." (Lk. 12:33). He told the parable of the rich farmer whose life centered in hoarding—and called him a fool (Lk. 12:16–21). He said that if we really want the kingdom of God we must, like a merchant in search of fine pearls, be willing to sell everything we have to get it (Mt. 13:45, 46). He called all who would follow Him to a joyful life of carefree unconcern for possessions: "Give to every one who begs from you; and of him who takes away your goods, do not ask them again" (Lk. 6:30).

Jesus spoke to the question of economics more than any other single social issue. If in a comparatively simple society our Lord would lay such strong emphasis upon the spiritual dangers of wealth, how much more should we who live in a highly affluent culture take seriously the economic question.

The epistles reflect the same concern. Paul said, "Those who desire to be rich fall into temptation, into a snare, into many senseless and hurtful desires that plunge men into ruin and destruction (1 Tim. 6:9). A bishop should not be a "lover of money" (1 Tim. 3:3). A deacon should not be "greedy for gain" (1 Tim. 3:8). The writer to the Hebrews counseled, "Keep your life free from love of money, and be content with what you have; for he has said, 'I will never fail you nor forsake you' " (Heb. 13:5). James blamed killings and wars on the lust for possessions: "You desire and do not have; so you kill. And you covet and cannot obtain; so you fight and wage war" (Jas. 4:1–2). Paul called covetousness idolatry and commanded the Corinthian church to exercise stern discipline against anyone guilty of greed (Eph. 5:5, 1 Cor. 5:11). He listed greed alongside adultery and thievery and declared that those who live in those things would not inherit the kingdom of God. Paul counseled the wealthy not to trust in their wealth but in God, and to share generously with others (1 Tim. 6:17–19).

Having said this I must hasten to add that God intends that we should have adequate material provision. There is misery today from a simple lack of provision, just as there is misery when people try to make a life out of provision. Forced poverty is evil and should be renounced. Nor does the Bible condone asceticism. Scripture declares consistently and forcefully that the creation is good and to be enjoyed.

Asceticism makes an unbiblical division between a good spiritual world and an evil material world and so finds salvation in paying as little attention as possible to the physical realm of existence.

Asceticism and simplicity are mutually incompatible. Occasional superficial similarities in practice must never obscure the radical difference between the two. Asceticism renounces possessions. Simplicity sets possessions in proper perspective. Asceticism can find no place for a "land flowing with milk and honey.'' Simplicity can rejoice in this gracious provision from the hand of God. Asceticism can find contentment only when it is abased. Simplicity knows contentment in both abasement and abounding (Phil. 4:12).

Simplicity is the only thing that can sufficiently reorient our lives so that possessions can be genuinely enjoyed without destroying us. Without simplicity we will either capitulate to the "mammon" spirit of this present evil age, or we will fall into an un-Christian legalistic asceticism. Both lead to idolatry. Both are spiritually lethal.

Scripture abounds in descriptions of the abundant material provision God gives His people. "For the Lord your God is bringing you into a good land . . . a land . . . in which you will lack nothing" (Deut. 8:7–9). It also abounds in warnings about the danger of provisions that are not kept in proper perspective. "Beware lest you say in your heart, 'My power and the might of my hand have gotten me this wealth' " (Deut. 8:17).

The Spiritual Discipline of simplicity provides the needed perspective. Simplicity sets us free to receive the provision of God as a gift that is not ours to keep, and that can be freely shared with others. Once we recognize that the Bible denounces the materialist and the ascetic with equal vigor, we are prepared to turn our attention to the framing of a Christian understanding of simplicity.

A Place to Stand

Archimedes declared, "Give me a place to stand and I will move the earth." Such a focal point is important in every Discipline but is acutely so with simplicity. Of all the Disciplines simplicity is the most visible and therefore the most open to corruption. The majority of Christians have never seriously wrestled with the problem of simplicity, conveniently ignoring Jesus' many words on the subject. The reason is simple: this Discipline directly challenges our vested interests in an affluent life-style. But those who take the biblical teaching on simplicity seriously are faced with severe temptations toward legalism. In the earnest attempt to give concrete expression to Jesus' economic teaching it is easy to mistake our expression of the teaching for the teaching. We wear this attire or buy that kind of house and canonize our choices as the simple life. This danger gives special importance to finding and clearly articulating an Archimedian focal point for simplicity.

We have such a focal point in the words of Jesus:

Therefore I tell you, do not be anxious about your life, what you shall eat or what you shall drink, nor about your body, what you shall put on. Is not life more than food, and the body more than clothing? Look at the birds of the air: they neither sow nor reap nor gather into barns, and yet your heavenly Father feeds them. Are you not of more value than they? And which of you by being anxious can add one cubit to his span of life? And why are you anxious about clothing? Consider the lilies of the field, how they grow; they neither toil nor spin; yet I tell you even Solomon in all his glory was not arrayed like one of these. But if God so clothes the grass of the field, which today is alive and tomorrow is thrown into the oven, will he not much more clothe you, O men of little faith? Therefore do not be anxious, saying, "What shall we eat?" or "What shall we drink?" or "What shall we wear?" For the Gentiles seek all these things; and your heavenly Father knows that you need them all. *But seek first his kingdom and his righteousness, and all these things shall be yours as well* (Mt. 6:25–33).

The central point for the Discipline of simplicity is to seek the kingdom of God and the righteousness of His kingdom *first*—and then everything necessary will come in its proper order. It is impossible to overestimate the importance of Jesus' insight at this point. Everything hinges upon maintaining the "first" thing as first. Nothing must come before the kingdom of God, including the desire for a simple life-style. Simplicity becomes idolatry when it takes precedence over seeking the kingdom. Søren Kierkegaard wrote:

"Seek ye first God's kingdom and his righteousness." What does this mean, what have I to do, or what sort of effort is it that can be said to seek or pursue the kingdom of God? Shall I try to get a job suitable to my talents and powers in order thereby to exert an influence? No, thou shalt *first* seek God's kingdom. Shall I then give all my fortune to the poor? No, thou shalt *first* seek God's kingdom. Shall I then go out to proclaim this teaching to the world? No, thou shalt *first* seek God's kingdom. But then in a certain sense it is nothing I shall do. Yes, certainly, in a certain sense it is nothing, become nothing before God, learn to keep silent; in this silence is the beginning, which is, *first* to seek God's kingdom. . . .[4]

Focus upon the kingdom produces the inward reality, and without the inward reality we will degenerate into legalistic trivia. Nothing else can be central. The desire to get out of the rat race cannot be central, the redistribution of the world's wealth cannot be central, the concern for ecology cannot be central. The only thing that can be central in the Spiritual Discipline of simplicity is to seek *first* God's kingdom and the righteousness, both personal and social, of that kingdom. Worthy as all other concerns may be, the moment *they* become the focus of our efforts they become idolatry. To center on them will inevitably draw us into declaring that our particular activity *is* Christian simplicity. And, in fact, when the kingdom of God is genuinely placed first, ecological concerns, the poor, the equitable distribution of wealth and many other things will be given their proper attention. The person who does not seek the kingdom first does not seek it at all, regardless of how worthy the idolatry that he or she has substituted for it.

As Jesus made so clear in our central passage, freedom from anxiety is one of the inward evidences of seeking the kingdom of God first. The inward reality of simplicity involves a life of joyful unconcern for possessions. Neither the greedy nor the miserly know that liberty. It has nothing to do with abundance of possessions or their lack. It is an inward spirit of trust. The sheer fact that a person is living without things is no guarantee that he or she is living in simplicity. Paul taught us that the love of money is the root of all evil, and often those who have it the least love it the most. It is possible for a person to be developing an outward life-style of simplicity and to be filled with anxiety. Conversely, wealth does not bring freedom from anxiety.

> For riches and abundance come hypocritically clad in sheep's clothing pretending to be security against anxieties and they become then the object of anxiety . . . they secure a man against anxieties just about as well as the wolf which is put to tending the sheep secures them . . . against the wolf. . . .[5]

Freedom from anxiety is characterized by three inner attitudes. If what we have we receive as a gift, and if what we have is to be cared for by God, and if what we have is available to others, then we will possess freedom from anxiety. *This is the inward reality of simplicity.* However, if what we have we believe we have gotten, and if what we have we believe we must hold onto, and if what we have is not available to others, then we will live in anxiety. Such persons will never know simplicity regardless of the outward contortions they may put themselves through in order to live "the simple life."

To receive what we have as a gift from God is the first inner attitude of simplicity. We work but we know that it is not our work that gives us what we have. We live by grace even when it comes to "daily bread." We are dependent upon God for the simplest elements of life: air, water, sun. What we have is not the result of our labor, but of the gracious care of God. When we are tempted to think that what we own is the result of our personal efforts, it takes only a little drought or a small accident to show us once again how radically dependent we are for everything.

To know that it is God's business, and not ours, to care for what we have is the second inner attitude of simplicity. God is able to protect what we possess. We can trust Him. Does that mean that we should never take the keys out of the car or lock the door? Of course not. But we know that the lock on the door is not what protects the house. It is only common sense to observe normal precaution, but if we believe that it is precaution that protects us and our goods we will be riddled with anxiety. There simply is no such thing as "burglar proof" precaution. Obviously these matters are not restricted to possessions but include such things as our reputation or our employment. Simplicity means the freedom to trust God for these (and all) things.

To have our goods available to others marks the third inner attitude of simplicity. Martin Luther said somewhere, "If our goods are not available to the community they are stolen goods." The reason we find these words so difficult is our fear of the future. We cling to our possessions rather than sharing them because we are anxious about tomorrow. But if we truly believe that God is who Jesus said He is, then we do not need to be afraid. When we come to see God as the almighty Creator *and* our loving Father we can share because we know that He will care for us. If someone is in need we are free to help them. Again, ordinary common sense will define the parameters of our sharing and save us from foolishness.

When we are seeking first the kingdom of God these three attitudes will characterize our lives. Taken together they define what Jesus meant by "do not be anxious." They comprise the inner reality of Christian Simplicity. And we can be certain that when we live in this central reality "all these things" that are necessary for abundant living will be ours as well.

The Outward Expression of Simplicity

To describe simplicity only as an inner reality is to say something false. The inner reality is not a reality until there is an outward expression. To experience the liberating spirit of simplicity *will* affect how we live. As I have warned earlier, to give specific application to simplicity runs the risk of deteriorating into legalistic rules. It is a risk, however, that I must take, for to refuse to discuss specifics would banish the Discipline to the theoretical. After all, the writers of Scripture constantly took that risk.*

I want to list ten controlling principles for the outward expression of simplicity. They should not be viewed as laws but as one attempt to flesh out the meaning of simplicity into twentieth-century life.

First, buy things for their usefulness rather than their status. Cars

---

* It is sad to realize that often the attempt of Scripture to apply the principle of simplicity to a given culture has been universalized by succeeding generations and turned into soul-killing laws. Witness, for example, the laws against Christians braiding their hair or wearing rings because Peter had said to the people of his day, "Let not yours be the outward adorning with braiding of hair, decoration of gold, and wearing of robes" (1 Pet. 3:3).

should be bought for their utility, not their prestige. Consider riding a bicycle. In building or buying homes, thought should be given to livability rather than how much it will impress others. Don't have more house than is reasonable. After all, who needs seven rooms for two people?

Consider your clothes. Most people have no need for more clothes. They buy more not because they need clothes, but because they want to keep up with the fashions. Hang the fashions. Buy only what you need. Wear your clothes until they are worn out. Stop trying to impress people with your clothes and impress them with your life. If it is practical in your situation, learn the joy of making clothes. And for God's sake (and I mean that quite literally) have clothes that are practical rather than ornamental. John Wesley declared, "As . . . for apparel, I buy the most lasting and, in general, the plainest I can. I buy no furniture but what is necessary and cheap." [6]

Second, reject anything that is producing an addiction in you. Learn to distinguish between a real psychological need, like cheerful surroundings, and an addiction. Eliminate or cut down on the use of addictive, nonnutritional drinks: alcohol, coffee, tea, Coca–Cola, etc. If you have become addicted to television, by all means sell your set or give it away. Any of the media that you find you cannot do without, get rid of: radios, stereos, magazines, movies, newspapers, books. Chocolate has become a serious addiction for many people. If money has a grip on your heart, give some away and feel the inner release. Simplicity is freedom, not slavery. Refuse to be a slave to anything but God.

Third, develop a habit of giving things away. If you find that you are becoming attached to some possession, consider giving it to someone who needs it. I still remember the Christmas I decided that rather than buying or even making an item for a particular individual I would give him something that meant a lot to me. My motive was selfish: I wanted to know the liberation that comes from even this simple act of voluntary poverty. The gift was a ten-speed bike. As I drove to his home to deliver the gift, I remember singing with new meaning the worship chorus, "Freely, freely you have received; freely, freely give." Yesterday my six-year-old son heard of a classmate who needs a lunch pail and asked me if he could give him his own lunch pail. Hallelujah!

De-accumulate. Masses of things that are not needed complicate life. They must be sorted and stored and dusted and re-sorted and re-stored ad nauseam. Most of us could get rid of half our possessions without any serious sacrifice. We would do well to follow the counsel of Thoreau: "Simplify, simplify."

Fourth, refuse to be propagandized by the custodians of modern gadgetry. Timesaving devices almost never save time. Beware of those words, "It will pay for itself in six months." Most gadgets are built to break down and wear out and so complicate our lives rather than enhance them. This problem is a plague in the toy industry. Our children do not need to be entertained by dolls that cry, eat, wet, sweat and spit. An old rag doll can be more enjoyable and more lasting. Often children find more joy out of playing with old pots and pans than the latest space set. Look for toys that are educational and durable. Make some yourself.

Usually gadgets are an unnecessary drain on the energy resources of the world. The United States has less than 6 percent of the world's population, but consumes about 33 percent of the world's energy. In the United States, air conditioners alone use the same amount of energy as does the entire country of China with its 830 million people.[7] Environmental responsibility alone should keep us from the majority of the gadgets produced today.

Propagandists try to convince us that because the newest model of this or that has a new feature (trinket?) we must sell the old one and buy the new one. Sewing machines have new stitches, tape recorders have new buttons, encyclopedias have new indexes. Such media dogma needs to be carefully scrutinized. Often "new" features are only a way of inducing us to buy what we do not need. Probably that refrigerator will serve us quite well for the rest of our lives even without the automatic ice maker and rainbow colors.

Fifth, learn to enjoy things without owning them. Owning things is an obsession in our culture. If we own it, we feel we can control it; and if we can control it, we feel it will give us more pleasure. The idea is an illusion. Many things in life can be enjoyed without possessing or controlling them. Share things. Enjoy the beach without feeling you have to buy a piece of it. Enjoy public parks and libraries.

Sixth, develop a deeper appreciation for the creation. Get close to the earth. Walk whenever you can. Listen to the birds—they are God's messengers. Enjoy the texture of grass and leaves. Marvel in the rich colors everywhere. Simplicity means to discover once again that "the earth is the Lord's and the fullness thereof" (Psa. 24:1).

Seventh, look with a healthy skepticism at all "buy now, pay later" schemes. They are a trap and serve to deepen your bondage. Both Old and New Testaments condemn usury for good reasons. ("Usury" in the Bible is not used in the modern sense of exorbitant interest; it referred to any interest at all.) Charging interest was viewed as an unbrotherly exploitation of another's misfortune, hence a denial of Christian community. Jesus denounced usury as a sign of the old life and admonished His disciples to "lend, expecting nothing in return" (Lk. 6:35).

These words of Scripture should not be construed into some kind of universal law obligatory upon all cultures at all times. But neither should they be thought of as totally irrelevant to modern society. Behind those biblical injunctions stand centuries of accumulated wisdom (and perhaps some bitter experiences!). Certainly prudence as well as simplicity would demand that we use extreme caution before incurring debt.

Eighth, obey Jesus' instructions about plain, honest speech. "Let what you say be simply 'Yes' or 'No'; anything more than this comes from evil" (Mt. 5:37). If you consent to do a task, do it. Avoid flattery and half-truths. Make honesty and integrity the distinguishing characteristics of your speech. Reject jargon and abstract speculation whose purpose is to obscure and impress rather than to illuminate and inform.

Plain speech is difficult because we so seldom live out of the divine Center, so seldom respond only to heavenly promptings. Often fear of what others may think or a hundred other motives determine our "yes" or "no" rather than obedience to divine urgings. Then if a more attractive opportunity, or a situation that will put us in a better light, arises we quickly reverse our decision. But if our speech comes out of obedience to the divine Center, we will find no reason to turn our "yes" into "no" and our "no" into "yes." We will be living in simplicity of speech because our words will have only one Source. Søren Kierkegaard wrote: "If thou art absolutely obedient to God, then there is no ambiguity in thee and . . . thou art mere simplicity before God . . . . One thing there is which all Satan's cunning and

all the snares of temptation cannot take by surprise, and that is simplicity."[8]

Ninth, reject anything that will breed the oppression of others. Perhaps no person has more fully embodied this principle than the eighteenth-century Quaker tailor John Woolman. His famous *Journal* is
redundant with tender references to his desire to live so as not to
oppress others.

> Here I was led into a close and laborious inquiry whether I, as
> an individual, kept clear from all things which tended to stir up
> or were connected with wars, either in this land or in Africa; my
> heart was deeply concerned that in future I might in all things
> keep steadily to the pure truth, and live and walk in the plainness
> and simplicity of a sincere follower of Christ . . . . And here
> luxury and coveteousness, with the numerous oppressions and
> other evils attending them, appeared very afflicting to me, and I
> felt in that which is immutable that the seeds of great calamity
> and desolation are sown and growing fast on this continent.[9]

That is one of the most difficult and sensitive issues for twentieth-century Christians to face, but face it we must. Do we sip our coffee and
eat our bananas at the expense of exploiting Latin American peasants?
In a world of limited resources, does our lust for wealth mean the poverty of others? Should we buy products that are made by forcing people into dull assembly-line jobs? Do we enjoy hierarchical relationships in the company or factory that keep others under us? Do we
oppress our children or spouse because certain tasks are beneath us?

Often our oppression is tinged with racism and sexism. The color of
the skin still affects one's position in the company. The sex of a job
applicant still affects the salary. May God give us prophets today who,
like John Woolman, will call us "from the desire of wealth" so that
we may be able to "break the yoke of oppression."[10]

Tenth, shun whatever would distract you from your main goal.
George Fox warned:

> But there is the danger and the temptation to you, of drawing
> your minds into your business, and clogging them with it; so that
> ye can hardly do anything to the service of God, but there will
> be crying, my business, my business; and your minds will go

into the things, and not over the things . . . . And then, if the
Lord God cross you, and stop you by sea and land, and take
your goods and customs from you, that your minds should not
be cumbered, then that mind that is cumbered, will fret, being
out of the power of God.[11]

God give us the courage, wisdom and strength always to hold as the
number-one priority of our lives to "seek first his kingdom and his
righteousness," understanding all that that implies. To do so is to live
in simplicity.

7. THE DISCIPLINE OF SOLITUDE

Settle yourself in solitude and you will come upon Him in yourself—Teresa of Avila

Jesus calls us from loneliness to solitude. The fear of being left alone petrifies people. A new child in the neighborhood sobs to his mother, "No one ever plays with me." A college freshman yearns for her high-school days when she was the center of attention: "Now, I'm a nobody." A business executive sits dejected in his office, powerful, yet alone. An old woman lies in a nursing home waiting to go "Home."

Our fear of being alone drives us to noise and crowds. We keep up a constant stream of words even if they are inane. We buy radios that strap to our wrist or fit over our ears so that if no one else is around at least we are not condemned to silence. T. S. Eliot analyzed our culture so well when he wrote, "Where shall the world be found, where will the word resound? Not here, there is not enough silence." [1]

But loneliness or clatter are not our only alternatives. We can cultivate an inner solitude and silence that sets us free from loneliness and fear. Loneliness is inner emptiness. Solitude is inner fulfillment. Solitude is not first a place but a state of mind and heart.

There is a solitude of the heart that can be maintained at all times. Crowds or the lack of them have little to do with this inward attentiveness. It is quite possible to be a desert hermit and never experience solitude. But if we possess inward solitude we will not fear being alone, for we know that we are not alone. Neither do we fear being with others, for they do not control us. In the midst of noise and confusion we are settled into a deep inner silence.

Inward solitude will have outward manifestations. There will be the freedom to be alone, not in order to be away from people but in order to hear better. Jesus lived in inward "heart solitude." He also frequently experienced outward solitude. He inaugurated His ministry by spending forty days alone in the desert (Mt. 4:1–11). Before He chose the twelve He spent the entire night alone in the desert hills (Lk. 6:12). When He received the news of the death of John the Baptist, He "withdrew from there in a boat to a lonely place apart" (Mt. 14:13). After the miraculous feeding of the five thousand Jesus made His disciples leave; then He dismissed the crowd and "went up into the hills by himself . . ." (Mt. 14:23). Following a long night of work "in the morning, a great while before day, he rose and went out to a lonely place . . ." (Mk. 1:35). When the twelve had returned from a preaching and healing mission, Jesus instructed them, "Come away by yourselves to a lonely place . . ." (Mk. 6:31). Following the healing of a leper Jesus "withdrew to the wilderness and prayed" (Lk. 5:16). With three disciples He sought out the silence of a lonely mountain as the stage for the transfiguration (Mt. 17:1–9). As he prepared for His highest and most holy work, Jesus sought the solitude of the garden of Gethsemane (Mt. 26:36–46). One could go on, but perhaps this is sufficient to show that the seeking out of a solitary place was a regular practice with Jesus. So it should be for us.

In *Life Together,* Dietrich Bonhoeffer titled one of his chapters "The Day Together" and perceptively titled the following chapter "The Day Alone." Both are essential for spiritual success. He wrote:

> Let him who cannot be alone beware of community. . . . Let him who is not in community beware of being alone. . . . Each by itself has profound pitfalls and perils. One who wants fellowship without solitude plunges into the void of words and feelings, and one who seeks solitude without fellowship perishes in the abyss of vanity, self-infatuation, and despair.[2]

Therefore we must seek out the recreating stillness of solitude if we want to be with others meaningfully. We must seek the fellowship and accountability of others if we want to be alone safely. We must cultivate both if we are to live in obedience.

Solitude and Silence

Without silence there is no solitude. Though silence sometimes involves the absence of speech it always involves the act of listening. Simply to refrain from talking, without a heart listening to God, is not silence.

> A day filled with noise and voices can be a day of silence, if the noises become for us the echo of the presence of God, if the voices are, for us, messages and solicitations of God. When we speak of ourselves and are filled with ourselves, we leave silence behind. When we repeat the intimate words of God that he has left within us, our silence remains intact.[3]

We must understand the connection between inner solitude and inner silence. The two are inseparable. All of the masters of the interior life speak of the two in the same breath. For example, *The Imitation of Christ* which has been the unchallenged masterpiece of devotional literature for five hundred years has a section titled "On the Love of Solitude and Silence." Dietrich Bonhoeffer makes the two an inseparable whole in *Life Together* as does Thomas Merton in *Thoughts in Solitude*. In fact, I wrestled for some time trying to decide whether to title this chapter the Discipline of solitude or the Discipline of silence, so closely connected are the two in all the great devotional literature. Of necessity, therefore, we must come to understand and experience the transforming power of silence if we are to know solitude.

There is an old proverb to the effect that "the man who opens his mouth, closes his eyes!" The purpose of silence and solitude is to be able to see and hear. Control rather than no noise is the key to silence. James saw clearly that the person who could control his tongue is perfect (Jas. 3:1–12). Under the Discipline of silence and solitude we learn when to speak and when to refrain from speaking. The person who views the Disciplines as laws will always turn silence into an absurdity: "I'll not speak for the next forty days!" This is always a severe temptation to any true disciple who wants to live under silence and solitude. Thomas à Kempis wrote: "It is easier to be silent altogether than to speak with moderation."[4] The wise preacher of Ecclesiastes said that there was "a time to keep silent and a time to speak" (Eccl. 3:7). Control is the key.

James's analogies of the rudder and the bridle suggest to us that the tongue guides as well as controls. The tongue guides our course in many ways. If we tell a lie we are led to telling more lies to cover up the first lie. Soon we are forced to behave in a certain way in order to give credence to the lie. No wonder James declares that "the tongue is a fire" (Jas. 3:6).

The disciplined person is the person who can do what needs to be done when it needs to be done. The mark of a championship basketball team is a team that can score the points when they are needed. Most of us can get the ball in the hoop eventually but we can't do it when it is needed. Likewise a person who is under the Discipline of silence is a person who can say what needs to be said when it needs to be said. "A word fitly spoken is like apples of gold in a setting of silver" (Prov. 25:11). If we are silent when we should speak, we are not living in the Discipline of silence. If we speak when we should be silent, we again miss the mark.

The Sacrifice of Fools

In Ecclesiastes we read "To draw near to listen is better than to offer the sacrifice of fools" (Eccl. 5:1). The sacrifice of fools is humanly initiated religious talk. The preacher continued, "Be not rash with your mouth, nor let your heart be hasty to utter a word before God, for God is in heaven, and you upon earth; therefore let your words be few" (Eccl. 5:2).

When Jesus took Peter, James and John up to the mountain and was transfigured before them, Moses and Elijah appeared and carried on a conversation with Jesus. The Greek text goes on to say, "And *answering,* Peter said to them . . . if you will I will make here three shelters . . ." (Mt. 17:4). That is so telling. No one was even speaking to Peter. He was offering the sacrifice of fools.

John Woolman's *Journal* contains a moving and tender account of learning control over the tongue. His words are so graphic that they are best quoted in full:

I went to meetings in an awful frame of mind, and endeavored to be inwardly acquainted with the language of the true Shepherd. One day, being under a strong exercise of spirit, I stood up and said some words in a meeting; but not keeping close to the Divine opening, I said more than was required of me. Being soon sensible of my error, I was afflicted in mind some weeks, without any light or comfort, even to that degree that I could not take satisfaction in anything. I remembered God, and was troubled, and in the depth of my distress he had pity upon me, and sent the Comforter. I then felt forgiveness for my offence; my mind became calm and quiet, and I was truly thankful to my gracious Redeemer for his mercies. About six weeks after this, feeling the spring of Divine love opened, and a concern to speak, I said a few words in a meeting, in which I found peace. Being thus humbled and disciplined under the cross, my understanding became more strengthened to distinguish the pure spirit which inwardly moves upon the heart, and which taught me to wait in silence sometimes many weeks together, until I felt that rise which prepares the creature to stand like a trumpet, through which the Lord speaks to his flock.[5]

What a description of the learning process one goes through in the Discipline of silence! Of particular significance was his increased ability from this experience to "distinguish the pure spirit which inwardly moves upon the heart."

One reason we can hardly bear to remain silent is that it makes us feel so helpless. We are so accustomed to relying upon words to manage and control others. If we are silent who will take control? God will take control; but we will never let Him take control until we trust Him. Silence is intimately related to trust.

The tongue is our most powerful weapon of manipulation. A frantic stream of words flows from us because we are in a constant process of adjusting our public image. We fear so deeply what we think other people see in us, so we talk in order to straighten out their understanding. If I have done some wrong thing and discover that you know about it I will be very tempted to help you understand my action! Silence is one of the deepest Disciplines of the Spirit simply because it puts the stopper on that.

One of the fruits of silence is the freedom to let our justification rest entirely with God. We don't need to straighten others out. There is a story of a medieval monk who was being unjustly accused of certain offenses. One day he looked out his window and watched a dog biting and tearing on a rug that had been hung out to dry. As he watched, the Lord spoke to him saying, "That is what I am doing to your reputation. But if you will trust Me you will not need to worry about the opinions of others." Perhaps more than anything else, silence brings us to believe that God can justify and set things straight.

George Fox often spoke of "the spirit of bondage" (Rom. 8:15, KJV) and how the world lay in that spirit. Frequently he would identify the spirit of bondage with the spirit of subservience to other human beings. In his *Journal* he would speak of "bringing people off of men," away from that spirit of bondage to law through other human beings. Silence is the chief means of bringing us into that liberation.

The tongue is a thermometer; it tells us our spiritual temperature. It is also a thermostat; it controls our spiritual temperature. Control of the tongue can mean everything. Have we been set free so that we can hold our tongue? Bonhoeffer wrote, "Real silence, real stillness, really holding one's tongue comes only as the sober consequence of spiritual stillness." [6] Dominic is reported to have visited Francis of Assisi and throughout the entire meeting neither spoke a single word. Only when we have learned to be truly silent are we enabled to speak the word that is needed *when* it is needed.

Catherine de Haeck Doherty has written, "All in me is silent and . . . . I am immersed in the silence of God." [7] It is in solitude that we come to experience the "silence of God" and so receive the inner silence that is the craving of our heart.

The Dark Night of the Soul

To take seriously the Discipline of solitude will mean at some point or points along the pilgrimage we will enter what St. John of the Cross vividly described as "the dark night of the soul." The "dark night" to which he calls us is not something bad or destructive. On the contrary it is an experience to be welcomed as a sick person might welcome a surgery that promises health and well-being. The purpose of the darkness is not to punish or afflict us. It is to set us free. St. John of the Cross embraced the soul's dark night as a divine appointment, a privi-

leged opportunity to draw close to the divine Center. He called the
dark night "sheer grace," adding:

> O guiding night!
> O night more lovely than the dawn!
> O night that has united
> The Lover with His beloved,
> Transforming the beloved in her Lover.[8]

What is involved in entering the dark night of the soul? It may be a
sense of dryness, depression, even lostness. It strips us of overdepen-
dence on the emotional life. The notion, often heard today, that such
experiences can be avoided and that we should live in peace and comfort, joy and celebration, only betrays the fact that much contemporary
experience is surface slush. The dark night is one of the ways God
brings us to a hush, a stillness, so that He may work an inner transformation upon the soul.

How is this dark night expressed in daily life? When solitude is
seriously pursued, there is usually a flush of initial success and then an
inevitable letdown—and with it a desire to abandon the pursuit altogether. Feelings leave and there is the sense that we are not getting
through to God. St. John of the Cross described it this way:

> . . . the darkness of the soul mentioned here . . . puts the sen-
> sory and spiritual appetites to sleep, deadens them, and deprives
> them of the ability to find pleasure in anything. It binds the
> imagination and impedes it from doing any good discursive
> work. It makes the memory cease, the intellect become dark and
> unable to understand anything, and hence it causes the will also
> to become arid and constrained, and all the faculties empty and
> useless. And over all this hangs a dense and burdensome cloud
> which afflicts the soul and keeps it withdrawn from God.[9]

In his poem "Canciones del Alma," St. John of the Cross twice
used the phrase, "My house being now all stilled." [10] In that graphic
line he indicated the importance of quieting all the physical, emotional, psychological, even spiritual senses. Every distraction of the
body, mind and spirit must be put into a kind of suspended animation
before this deep work of God upon the soul can occur. The ether must

take effect before the surgery can be performed. There comes inner silence, peace, stillness. During such a time of darkness, Bible reading, sermons, intellectual debate—all will fail to move or excite.

When God lovingly draws us into a dark night of the soul, there is often a temptation to blame everyone and everything for our inner dullness and to seek release from it. The preacher is such a bore. The hymn singing is so weak. We may begin to look around for another church or a new experience to give us "spiritual goose bumps." That is a serious mistake. Recognize the dark night for what it is. Be grateful that God is lovingly drawing you away from every distraction so that you can see Him. Rather than chafing and fighting, become still and wait.

I am not here speaking about dullness to spiritual things that comes as a result of sin or disobedience. I am speaking of the person who is seeking hard after God and who harbors no known sin in his heart.

> Who among you fears the Lord
>   and obeys the voice of his servant,
> *who walks in darkness*
>   *and has no light,*
> yet trusts in the name of the Lord
>   and relies upon his God? (Is. 50:10)

The point of the biblical passage is that it is quite possible to fear, obey, trust and rely upon the Lord and still "walk in darkness and have no light." You are living in obedience but you have entered a dark night of the soul.

St. John of the Cross indicated that during this experience there is a gracious protection from vices and a wonderful advance in the things of the kingdom of God.

> If a person at the time of these darknesses observes closely, he will see clearly how little the appetites and faculties are distracted with useless and harmful things and how secure he is from vainglory, from pride and presumption, from an empty and false joy, and from many other evils. By walking in darkness the soul not only avoids going astray but advances rapidly, because it thus gains the virtues.[11]

What should we do during such a time of inward affliction? First, disregard the advice of well-meaning friends to snap out of it. They do not understand what is occurring. Our age is so ignorant of such things that I do not recommend that you even talk about these matters. Above all, do not try to explain or justify why you may be "out of sorts." God is your justifier; rest your case with Him. If you can actually withdraw to a "desert place" for a season, do so. If not, go about your daily tasks. But whether in the "desert" or at home, hold in your heart a deep, inner, listening silence—and there be still until the work of solitude is done.

Perhaps St. John of the Cross has been leading us into deeper waters than we care to go. Certainly he is talking about a realm that most of us see only "through a glass darkly." Yet we do not need to censure ourselves for our timidity to scale these snowy peaks of the soul. These matters are best approached cautiously. But perhaps he has stirred within us a drawing toward higher, deeper experiences, no matter how slight the tug. It is like opening the door of our lives to this realm ever so slightly. That is all God asks, and all He needs.

To conclude our journey into the dark night of the soul, let us ponder these powerful words of our spiritual mentor:

> Oh, then, spiritual soul, when you see your appetites darkened, your inclinations dry and constrained, your faculties incapacitated for any interior exercise, do not be afflicted; think of this as a grace, since God is freeing you from yourself and taking from you your own activity. However well your actions may have succeeded you did not work so completely, perfectly, and securely—owing to their impurity and awkwardness—as you do now that God takes you by the hand and guides you in darkness, as though you were blind, along a way and to a place you know not. You would never have succeeded in reaching this place no matter how good your eyes and your feet.[12]

Steps Into Solitude

The Spiritual Disciplines are things that we do. We must never lose sight of that fact. It is one thing to talk piously about "the solitude of the heart" but if that does not somehow work its way into our experience then we have missed the point of the Disciplines. We are dealing with actions, not merely states of mind. It is not enough to say, "Well, I am most certainly in possession of inner solitude and silence; there is nothing that I need to do." All those who have come into the living silences have done certain things, have ordered their lives in a particular way, so as to receive this "peace that passes all understanding." If we are to succeed we must pass beyond the theoretical into life situations.

What are some steps into solitude? The first thing we can do is to take advantage of the "little solitudes" that fill our day. Consider the solitude of those early morning moments in bed before the family awakens. Think of the solitude of a morning cup of coffee before beginning the work of the day. There is the solitude of bumper to bumper traffic during the freeway rush hour. There can be little moments of rest and refreshment when we turn a corner and see a flower or a tree. Instead of vocal prayer before a meal consider inviting everyone to join into a few moments of gathered silence. Once while driving a carload of chattering children and adults, I exclaimed, "Let's play a game and see if we can all be absolutely quiet until we reach the airport" (about five minutes away). It worked, blessedly so. Find new joy and meaning in the little walk from the subway to your home. Slip outside just before bed and taste the silent night.

These tiny snatches of time are often lost to us. What a pity! They can and should be redeemed. They are times for inner quiet, for reorienting our lives like a compass needle. They are little moments that help us to be genuinely present where we are.

What else can we do? We can find or develop a "quiet place" designed for silence and solitude. Homes are being built constantly. Why not insist that a little inner sanctuary be put into the plans, a small place where any family member could go to be alone and silent? What's to stop us? The money? We build elaborate play rooms and family rooms and think it well worth the expense. If you already own a home consider enclosing a little section of the garage or patio. If you live in an apartment be creative and find other ways to allow for solitude. I know of one family that has a special chair; whenever anyone sits in it he or she is saying, "Please don't bother me, I want to be alone."

Find places outside your home: a spot in a park, a church sanctuary (that keeps its doors unlocked), even a storage closet somewhere. A retreat center near us has built a lovely one-person cabin specifically for private meditation and solitude. It is called "The Quiet Place." Churches invest millions of dollars in buildings. How about building one place where an individual can come to be alone for several days? Catherine de Haeck Doherty has pioneered in developing *Poustinias* (a Russian word meaning "desert") in North America. These are places specifically designed for solitude and silence.*

In the chapter on study we considered the importance of observing ourselves to see how often our speech is a frantic attempt to explain and justify our actions. Having seen this in yourself, experiment with doing deeds without any words of explanation whatever. Note your sense of fear that people will misunderstand why you have done what you have done. Try to allow God to be your justifier.

Discipline yourself so that your words are few and full. Become known as a person who has something to say when you speak. Maintain plain speech. Do what you say you will do. "It is better that you should not vow than that you should vow and not pay" (Eccl. 5:5). When our tongue is under our authority the words of Bonhoeffer become true of us: "Much that is unnecessary remains unsaid. But the essential and the helpful thing can be said in a few words." [13]

Go another step. Try to live one entire day without words at all. Do it not as a law but as an experiment. Note your feelings of helplessness and excessive dependence upon words to communicate. Try to find new ways to relate to others that are not dependent upon words. Enjoy, savor the day. Learn from it.

Four times a year withdraw for three to four hours for the purpose of reorienting your life goals. This can easily be done in one evening. Stay late at your office or do it at home or find a quiet corner in a public library. Reevaluate your goals and objectives in life. What do you want to have accomplished one year from now? Ten years from now? Our tendency is highly to overestimate what we can accomplish in one year and highly underestimate what we can accomplish in ten years. Set realistic goals but be willing to dream, to stretch. (This book was a dream in my mind for several years before it became a reality.) In the quiet of those brief hours, listen to the thunder of God's silence. Keep a journal record of what comes to you.

---

*The story of the development of these centers is described in her book, *Poustinia: Christian Spirituality of the East for Western Man* (Notre Dame: Ave Maria Press, 1976).

Reorientation and goal-setting do not need to be cold and calculating, as some suppose, done with a marketing-analysis mentality. Perhaps as you enter into a listening silence the delightful impression emerges to learn this year how to weave or how to make pottery. Does that sound too earthy, too unspiritual a goal? God is intently interested in such matters. Are you? Maybe you will want to learn (experience) more about the spiritual gifts of miracles, healing and tongues. Or you may do as one friend I know who is spending large periods of time experiencing the gift of helps, learning to be a servant. Perhaps this next year you would like to read all the writings of C. S. Lewis or D. Elton Trueblood. Maybe in five years from now you would like to be qualified to work with handicapped children. Does choosing these goals sound like a salesperson's manipulation game? Of course not. It is merely setting a direction for your life. You are going to go somewhere, so how much better to have a direction that has been set by communion with the divine Center.

Under the Discipline of study we explored the idea of study retreats of two to three days in duration. Such experiences are heightened when they are combined with an inner immersion into the silence of God. Like Jesus we must go away from people so that we can be truly present when we are with people. Take a retreat once a year for no other purpose in mind but solitude.

The fruit of solitude is increased sensitivity and compassion for others. There comes a new freedom to be with people. There is new attentiveness to their needs, new responsiveness to their hurts. Thomas Merton observed:

> It is in deep solitude that I find the gentleness with which I can truly love my brothers. The more solitary I am the more affection I have for them. It is pure affection and filled with reverence for the solitude of others. Solitude and silence teach me to love my brothers for what they are, not for what they say. [14]

Don't you feel a tug, a yearning to sink down into the silence and solitude of God? Don't you long for something more? Doesn't every breath crave a deeper, fuller exposure to His Presence? It is the Discipline of solitude that will open the door. You are welcome to come in and "listen to God's speech in his wondrous, terrible, gentle, loving, all-embracing silence." [15]

8. THE DISCIPLINE OF SUBMISSION

A Christian man is the most free lord of all, and subject to none; a Christian man is the most dutiful servant of all, and subject to everyone. —*Martin Luther*

Of all the Spiritual Disciplines none has been more abused than the Discipline of submission. Somehow the human species has an extraordinary knack for taking the best teaching and turning it to the worst ends. Nothing can put people into bondage like religion, and nothing in religion has done more to manipulate and destroy people than a deficient teaching on submission. Therefore we must work our way through this Discipline with great care and discernment in order to insure that we are the ministers of life, not death.

Every Discipline has its corresponding freedom. If I have schooled myself in the art of rhetoric I am free to deliver a moving speech when the occasion requires it. Demosthenes was free to be an orator only because he had gone through the discipline of speaking above the ocean roar with pebbles in his mouth. The purpose of the Disciplines is freedom. Our aim is the freedom, not the Discipline. The moment we make the Discipline our central focus we will turn it into law and lose the corresponding freedom.

The Disciplines in themselves are of no value whatever. They have value only as a means of setting us before God so that He can give us the liberation we seek. The liberation is the end; the Disciplines are *merely* the means. They are not the answer; they only lead us to the Answer. We must clearly understand this limitation of the Disciplines if we are to avoid bondage. Not only must we understand but we need to underscore it to ourselves again and again, so severe is our temptation to center on the Disciplines. Let us forever center on Christ and view the Spiritual Disciplines as a way of drawing us closer to His heart.

The Freedom in Submission

I said that every Discipline has its corresponding freedom. What freedom corresponds to submission? It is the ability to lay down the terrible burden of always needing to get our own way. The obsession to demand that things go the way we want them to go is one of the greatest bondages in human society today. People will spend weeks, months, even years in a perpetual stew because some little thing did not go as they wished. They will fuss and fume. They will get mad about it. They will act as if their very life hangs on the issue. They may even get an ulcer over it.

In the Discipline of submission we are released to drop the matter, to forget it. Frankly, most things in life are not nearly so important as we think they are. Our lives will not come to an end if this or that does not happen.

If you will watch these things you will see, for example, that almost all church fights and splits occur because people do not have the freedom to give in to each other. We insist that a critical issue is at stake; we are fighting for a sacred principle. Perhaps that is true. Usually it is not. Often we cannot stand to give in simply because it would mean that we would not get things our own way. Only in submission are we enabled to bring that spirit to a place where it no longer controls us. Only submission can free us sufficiently to enable us to distinguish between genuine issues and stubborn self-will.

If we could only come to see that most things in life are not major issues, then we could hold them lightly. We discover that they are no big deal. So often we say, "Well, I don't care," when what we really mean (and what we convey to others) is that we care a great deal. It is precisely here that the Discipline of silence fits in so well with all the other Disciplines. Usually the best way to handle most matters of submission is to say nothing. There is the need for an all-encompassing spirit of grace beyond any kind of language or action. When we do so we set others and ourselves free.

The biblical teaching on submission focuses primarily on the spirit with which we view other people. Scripture is not attempting to set forth a series of hierarchical relationships but to communicate to us an inner attitude of mutual subordination. Peter, for example, called upon the slaves of his day to live in submission to their masters (1 Pet. 2:18). The counsel seems unnecessary until we realize that it is quite possible to obey a master without living in a spirit of submission to him. Outwardly we can do what people ask and inwardly be in rebellion against them. That concern for a spirit of consideration toward others pervades the entire New Testament. The old covenant stipulated that we must not murder. Jesus, however, stressed that the real issue was the inner spirit of murder with which we view people. With the matter of submission the same is true; the real issue is the spirit of consideration and deference we have when we are with others.

In submission we are at last free to value other people. Their dreams and plans become important to us. We have entered into a new, wonderful, glorious freedom, the freedom to give up our own rights for the good of others. For the first time we can love people unconditionally. We have given up the right for them to return our love. No longer do we feel that we have to be treated in a certain way. We can rejoice with their successes. We feel genuine sorrow at their failures. It is of little consequence that our plans are frustrated, if their plans succeed. We discover that it is far better to serve our neighbor than to have our own way.

Do you know what a liberation it is to give up your rights? It means you are set free from that seething anger and bitterness you feel when someone doesn't act toward you the way you feel they should. It means that at last you are able to break that vicious law of commerce which says, "You scratch my back, I'll scratch your back; you bloody my nose, I'll bloody your nose." It means freedom to obey Jesus' command, "Love your enemies and pray for those who persecute you" (Mt. 5:44). It means that for the first time we understand how it is possible to surrender the right to retaliate: "If any one strikes you on the right cheek, turn to him the other also" (Mt. 5:39).

A Touchstone

As you perhaps have noted, I have been coming at the matter of submission through the back door. I began by explaining what it does for us before defining what it is. That has been done for a purpose. Most of us have been exposed to such a mutilated form of biblical submission that either we have embraced the deformity or we have rejected the Discipline altogether. To do the former leads to self-hatred; to do the latter leads to arrogance. Before we become hung on the horns of this dilemma, let's consider a third alternative.

The touchstone for the biblical understanding of submission is Mark 8:34, "And he called to him the multitude with his disciples, and said to them, 'If any man would come after me, let him deny himself and take up his cross and follow me.' " Almost instinctively we draw back from these words. We are much more comfortable with words like "self-fulfillment" and "self-actualization" than we are with the thought of "self-denial." (In reality, Jesus' teaching on self-denial is the only thing that will genuinely bring self-fullfillment and self-actualization.) Self-denial conjures up in our minds all sorts of images of groveling and self-hatred. We imagine that it most certainly means the rejection of our individuality and will probably lead to various forms of self-mortification.

On the contrary, Jesus called us to self-denial without self-hatred. Self-denial is simply a way of coming to understand that we do not have to have our own way. Our happiness is not dependent upon getting what we want.

Self-denial does not mean the loss of our identity as some suppose. Without our identity we could not even be subject to each other. Did Jesus lose His identity when He set His face toward Golgotha? Did Peter lose his identity when he responded to Jesus' cross-bearing command, "Follow me" (Jn. 21:19)? Did Paul lose his identity when he committed himself to the One who had said, "I will show him how much he must suffer for the sake of my name" (Acts 9:16)? Of course not. We know that the opposite was true. They found their identity in the act of self-denial.

Self-denial is not the same thing as self-contempt. Self-contempt claims that we have no worth, and even if we did have worth we should reject it. Self-denial declares that we are of infinite worth and shows us how to realize it. Self-contempt denies the goodness of the creation; self-denial affirms that it was indeed good. Jesus made the ability to love ourselves the prerequisite for our reaching out to others (Mt. 22:39). Self-love and self-denial are not in conflict. Jesus made it quite clear more than once that self-denial is the only sure way to love ourselves. "He who finds his life will lose it, and he who loses his life for my sake will find it" (Mt. 10:39).

Again, we must underscore to ourselves that self-denial means the freedom to give way to others. It means to hold others' interests above self-interest. In this way self-denial releases us from self-pity. When we live outside of self-denial we demand that things go our way. When they do not we revert to self-pity. "Poor me!" Outwardly we may submit but we do so in a spirit of martyrdom. This spirit of self-pity, of martyrdom, is a sure sign that the Discipline of submission has gone to seed. That is why self-denial is the basis for this Discipline; it saves us from self-pity.

Modern men and women find it extremely difficult to read the great devotional masters because they make such lavish use of the language of self-denial. It is hard for us to be open to the words of Thomas à Kempis, "To have no opinion of ourselves, and to think always well and highly of others, is great wisdom and perfection." [1] We struggle to listen to the words of Jesus, "If any man would come after me, let him deny himself and take up his cross and follow me" (Mk. 8:34). This is all because we have failed to understand Jesus' teaching that the way to self-fulfillment is through self-denial. To save the life is to lose it; to lose it for Christ's sake is to save it (Mk. 8:35). George Matheson set into the hymnody of the church this wonderful paradox of fulfillment through self-denial:

> Make me a captive, Lord,
> And then I shall be free;
> Force me to render up my sword,
> And I shall conqueror be.
> I sink in life's alarms
> When by myself I stand;
> Imprison me within Thine arms,
> And strong shall be my hand. [2]

Perhaps the air has been sufficiently cleared so that we can look upon self-denial as the liberation that it really is. We must be convinced of this for, as has been stated, self-denial is the touchstone for the Discipline of submission.

Revolutionary Subordination as Taught by Jesus*

The most radical social teaching of Jesus was His total reversal of the contemporary notion of greatness. Leadership is found in becoming the servant of all. Power is discovered in submission. The foremost symbol of this radical servanthood is the cross. "He [Jesus] humbled himself and became obedient unto death, even death on a cross" (Phil. 2:8). But note this: Christ not only died a cross-death, He lived a cross-life. The way of the cross, the way of a suffering servant, was essential to His ministry. Jesus lived the cross-life in submission to His fellow human beings. He was the servant of all. He flatly rejected the cultural givens of position and power when He said, "You are not to be called rabbi. . . . Neither be called masters" (Mt. 23:8-10). Jesus shattered the customs of His day when He lived out the cross-life by taking women seriously and by being willing to meet with children. He lived the cross-life when He took a towel and washed the feet of His disciples. This Jesus who easily could have called down a legion of angels to His aid chose instead the cross-death of Calvary. Jesus' life was the cross-life of submission and service. Jesus' death was the cross-death of conquest by suffering.

It is impossible to overstate the revolutionary character of Jesus' life and teaching at this point. It did away with all the claims to privileged position and status. It called into being a whole new order of leadership. The cross-life of Jesus undermined all social orders based on power and self-interest.†

As I noted earlier Jesus called His followers to live the cross-life. "If any man would come after me, let him deny himself and take up his cross and follow me" (Mk. 8:34). He flatly told His disciples, "If

---

* I am endebted to John Howard Yoder for this term and for several of the ideas listed under it. His book, *The Politics of Jesus* (Eerdmans, 1972), contains an excellent chapter on Revolutionary Subordination.

† The church today has failed to understand or if it understands has failed to obey, the implications of the cross-life for human society. Guy Hershberger has courageously explored some of these implications in his book, *The Way of the Cross in Human Relations* (Herald Press, 1958). He discusses how the way of servanthood should affect such issues as war, capitalism, trade unions, labor unions, materialism, employer-employee relations, race relations and others. (I am indebted to Hershberger for the term "cross-life.")

any one would be first, he must be last of all and servant of all" (Mk. 9:35). When Jesus immortalized the principle of the cross-life by washing the disciples' feet He added, "I have given you an example, that you also should do as I have done to you" (Jn. 13:15).

The cross-life is the life of voluntary submission. The cross-life is the life of freely accepted servanthood.

Revolutionary Subordination as Taught in the Epistles

Jesus' example and call to follow the way of the cross in all human relationships form the basis for the teaching of the epistles on submission. The apostle Paul grounds the imperative to the church to "count others better than yourselves" in the submission and self-denial of the Lord for our salvation. "He . . . emptied himself, taking the form of a servant" (Phil. 2:4–7). The apostle Peter in the middle of his instructions on submission directly appealed to the example of Jesus as the reason for submission. "For to this you have been called, because Christ also suffered for you, leaving you an example that you should follow in his steps. . . . When he was reviled, he did not revile in return; when he suffered, he did not threaten; but he trusted to him who judges justly" (1 Pet. 2:21–23). As a preface to the Ephesian *Haustafel** we read, "Be subject to one another *out of reverence for Christ*" (Eph. 5:21). The call for Christians to live the cross-life is rooted in the cross-life of Jesus Himself.

The Discipline of submission has been terribly misconstrued and abused from failure to see this wider context. Submission is an ethical theme that runs the gamut of the New Testament. It is a posture obligatory upon *all* Christians: men as well as women, fathers as well as children, masters as well as slaves. We are commanded to live a life of submission because Jesus lived a life of submission, not because we are in a particular place or station in life. Self-denial is a posture fitting those who follow the crucified Lord. Everywhere in the *Haustafel* the one and only compelling reason for submission is the example of Jesus.

* A term coined by Martin Luther meaning literally "house-table," hence a table of rules for the Christian household. The *Haustafel* has come to be recognized as a particular literary form and can be found in Ephesians 5:21ff., Colossians 3:18ff., Titus 2:4ff., and 1 Peter 2:18ff.

This singular rationale for submission is staggering when we compare it to other first-century writings. In them there was a constant appeal to submission because that was the way the gods had created things; it was one's station in life. Not a single New Testament writer appeals to submission on that basis. The teaching is revolutionary. They completely ignored all the contemporary customs of super-ordinate and sub-ordinate and called everyone to "count others better than yourselves" (Phil. 2:3).

The epistles first call to subordination those who by virtue of the given culture are already subordinate. "Wives, be subject to your husbands. . . . Children, obey your parents. . . . Slaves, obey in everything those who are your earthly masters . . ." (Col. 3:18–22 and parallels). The revolutionary thing about this teaching is that these people, to whom first-century culture afforded no choice at all are addressed as free moral agents. Paul gave personal moral responsibility to those who had no legal or moral status in their culture. He makes decision-makers of people who were forbidden to make decisions.

It is astonishing that Paul called them to subordination, since they were already subordinate by virtue of their place in first-century culture. The only meaningful reason for such a command was the fact that by virtue of the gospel message they had come to see themselves as free from a subordinate status in society. The gospel had challenged all second-class citizenships and they knew it. Paul urged voluntary subordination not because it was their station in life but because it was "fitting in the Lord" (Col. 3:18).

This feature of addressing moral teaching to the cultural subordinates is also a radical contrast to the contemporary literature of the day. The Stoics, for example, addressed *only* the person on the top side of the social order, encouraging him to do a good job in the super-ordinate position he already saw as his place. But Paul spoke first to the people that his culture said should not even be addressed and called them to the cross-life of Jesus.

Next the epistles turn to the culturally dominant partner in the relationship and also call him to the cross-life of Jesus. The imperative to subordination is reciprocal. "Husbands, love your wives. . . . Fathers, do not provoke your children. . . . Masters, treat your slaves justly and fairly . . ." (Col. 3:19–4:1 and parallels). It will most certainly be objected that the command to the dominant partner does not use the language of submission. What we fail to see is how much submission those commands demanded of the dominant partner in his cultural setting. For a first-century husband, father and master to obey Paul's injunction would make a dramatic difference in his behavior. The first-century wife, child and slave would not need to change one whit to follow Paul's command. If anything the sting of the teaching falls upon the dominant partner.[3]

Further we need to see that those imperatives to husbands, fathers and masters constitute another form of self-denial. They are just another set of words to convey the same truth, namely, that we can be set free from the need to have things our own way. If a husband loves his wife he will live in consideration of her needs. He will be willing to give in to her, to submit to her. He is freed to regard her as higher than himself. He can look to the needs of his children and regard them as higher than himself (Phil. 2:3).

In Ephesians Paul exhorted slaves to live in a spirit of joyful, voluntary, willing service to their earthly masters. Then he exhorted masters, "Do the same to them" (Eph. 6:9). Such a thought was incredible to first-century ears. Slaves were thought to be chattel, not human beings. Yet Paul with divine authority counseled masters to give way to the needs of their slaves.

Perhaps the most perfect illustration of revolutionary subordination is Paul's tiny letter to Philemon. Onesimus, Philemon's runaway slave, had become a Christian. He was voluntarily returning to Philemon as part of what it meant for him to be a disciple of Christ. Paul urged Philemon to welcome Onesimus "no longer as a slave but more than a slave, as a beloved brother" (Philemon 16). John Yoder remarks, "This amounts to Paul's instructing Philemon, in the kind of noncoercive instruction which is fitting for a Christian brother, . . . that Onesimus is to be set free."[4] Onesimus was to be subordinate to Philemon by returning. Philemon was to be subordinate to Onesimus by setting him free. Both were to be mutually subordinate out of reverence for Christ (Eph. 5:21).

The epistles did not consecrate the existing hierarchical social structure. By making the command to subordination universal they relativized and undercut it. They called for Christians to live as citizens of a new order—and the most fundamental feature of this new order is universal subordination.

The Limits of Submission

The limits of the Discipline of submission are at the points at which it becomes destructive. It then becomes a denial of the law of love as taught by Jesus and is an affront to genuine biblical submission (Mt. 5, 6, 7 and especially 22:37–39).

Peter called Christians to radical submission to the state when he wrote, "Be subject for the Lord's sake to every human institution, whether it be the emperor as supreme, or to governors . . ." (1 Pet. 2:13, 14). Yet when the properly authorized government of his day commanded the infant church to stop proclaiming Christ, it was Peter who answered, "Whether it is right in the sight of God to listen to you rather than to God, you must judge; for we cannot but speak of what we have seen and heard" (Acts 4:19, 20). Upon a similar occasion Peter stated simply, "We must obey God rather than men" (Acts 5:29).

Understanding the cross-life of Jesus, Paul said, "Let every person be subject to the governing authorities" (Rom. 13:1). When Paul, however, saw that the state was failing to fulfill its God-ordained function of providing justice for all, he called it to account and insisted that the wrong be righted (Acts 16:37).

Were these men in opposition to their own principle of self-denial and submission? No. They simply understood that submission reaches the end of its tether when it becomes destructive. In fact, they illustrated revolutionary subordination by meekly refusing a destructive command and being willing to suffer the consequences. The German thinker Johannes Hamel has said that subordination includes "the possibility of a spirit-driven resistance, of an appropriate disavowal and a refusal ready to accept suffering at this or that particular point."[5]

Sometimes the limits of submission are easy to see. A wife is asked to beat her child unreasonably. A child is asked to aid an adult in an unlawful practice. A citizen is asked to violate the dictates of Scripture and conscience for the sake of the state. In each case the disciple refuses, not arrogantly but in a spirit of meekness and submission.

Often the limits of submission are extremely hard to define. What about the marriage partner who feels stifled and kept from personal fulfillment because of the professional career of the spouse? Is this a legitimate form of self-denial or is it destructive? What about the teacher who unjustly grades a student? Does the student submit or resist? What about the employer who promotes his employees on the basis of favoritism and vested interests? What does the deprived employee do, especially if the raise is needed for the good of his or her family?

These are extremely complicated questions simply because human relationships are complicated. They are questions that do not yield to simplistic answers. There is no such thing as a law of submission that will cover every situation. We must become highly skeptical of all laws that purport to handle every circumstance. Casuistic ethics always fail.

It is not an evasion of the issue to say that in defining the limits of submission we are thrown upon a deep dependence upon the Holy Spirit. After all, if we had a book of rules to cover every circumstance in life we would not need dependence. The Spirit is an accurate discerner of the thoughts and intents of the heart, both theirs and ours. He will be to us a present Teacher and Prophet and instruct us what to do in every situation.

The Acts of Submission

Submission and service function concurrently. Hence a great deal of the practical outflow of submission will come in the next chapter. There are, however, seven acts of submission that should be given brief comment.

The first act of submission is to the Triune God. At the beginning of the day we wait before Father, Son and Holy Spirit, in the words of the hymn writer, "yielded and still." The first words of our day form the prayer of Thomas à Kempis, "As thou wilt; what thou wilt; when thou wilt." [6] We yield our body, mind and spirit for His purposes. Likewise the day is lived in deeds of submission interspersed with constant ejaculations of inward surrender. As the first words of the morning are of submission so are the last words of the night. We surrender our body, mind and spirit into the hands of God to do with us as He pleases through the long darkness.

The second act of submission is to the Scripture. As we submit ourselves to the Word of God living (Jesus), so we submit ourselves to the Word of God written (Scripture). We yield ourselves first to hear the Word, second to receive the Word and third to obey the Word. We look to the Spirit who inspired the Scriptures to interpret and apply them to our condition. The word of Scripture, animated by the Holy Spirit, lives with us throughout the day.

The third act of submission is to our family. The dictum for the household should be "Let each of you look not only to his own interests, but also to the interests of others" (Phil. 2:4). Freely and graciously the members of the family make allowance for each other. The primary deed of submission is a commitment to listen to the other family members. Its corollary is a willingness to share, which is itself a work of submission.

The fourth act of submission is to our neighbors and those we meet in the course of our daily lives. The life of simple goodness is lived before them. If they are in need we help them. We perform small acts of kindness and ordinary neighborliness: sharing our food, baby-sitting their children, mowing their lawn, taking a moment to visit, sharing our tools. No task is too small, too trifling, for each one is an opportunity to live in submission.

The fifth act of submission is to the believing community, the body of Christ. If there are jobs to be filled and tasks to be done, we look at them closely to see if they are God's invitation to the cross-life. We cannot do everything but we can do some things. Sometimes these are matters of an organizational nature but most frequently they are spontaneous opportunities for little tasks of servanthood. There may at times come calls to serve the church universal and if the ministry is confirmed in our hearts we can submit to it with assurance and reverence.

The sixth act of submission is to the broken and despised. In every culture there are the "widows and orphans"; that is, the helpless, the undefended (Jas. 1:27). Our first responsibility is to be among them. Like Francis of Assisi in the thirteenth century and Kagawa in the twentieth, we must discover ways genuinely to identify with the downtrodden, the rejected. There we must live the cross-life.

The seventh act of submission is to the world. We live in an inter-
dependent international community. We cannot live in isolation. Our
environmental responsibility, or the lack of it, affects not only the people around the world but generations yet to be born. Starving nations
affect us. Our act of submission is a determination to live as a respon-
sible member of an increasingly irresponsible world.

A Final Note

In our day there has arisen a special problem about submission as it
relates to authority. The phenomenon which I am about to describe is
something I have observed repeatedly. When people begin to move
into the spiritual realm they see that Jesus is teaching a concept of authority that runs completely counter to the thinking of the systems of
this world. They come to perceive that authority does not reside in
positions, or degrees, or titles, or tenure, or *any* outward symbol. The
way of Christ is in another direction altogether: the way of spiritual
authority. Spiritual authority is God-ordained and God-sustained.
Human institutions may acknowledge this authority or they may not; it
makes no difference. The person with spiritual authority may have an
outward position of authority or may not; again, it makes no difference. Spiritual authority is marked by both compassion and power.
Those who walk in the Spirit can identify it immediately. They know
without question that submission is due the word that has been given
in spiritual authority.

But, and here is the difficulty, what about people who are in "positions of authority" but do not possess spiritual authority? Since Jesus
made it clear that the position does not give the authority, should this
person be obeyed? Can we not rather disregard all humanly ordained
authority and look for and submit only to spiritual authority? These are
the kinds of questions raised by persons who sincerely want to walk in
the way of the Spirit. The questions are legitimate and deserve a
careful answer.

The answer is not simple but neither is it impossible. *Revolutionary
subordination would command us to live in submission to human authority until it becomes destructive.** Both Peter and Paul called for

---

* See the section on "The Limits of Submission."

obedience to the pagan state because they understood the great good that resulted from this human institution. I have found that human "authorities" often have a great deal of wisdom that we neglect only at our peril.

To this I shall add another reason of my own why we should submit to persons in positions of authority who do not know spiritual authority. We should do so out of common courtesy and out of compassion for the person in that difficult predicament. I have a deep empathy for individuals in that plight for I have been there myself more than once. It is a frustrating, almost desperate, quagmire to be in a position of authority and to know that your roots are not deep enough into the divine life to command spiritual authority. I know the frantic feeling that makes a person strut and puff and devise clever gimmicks to manipulate people into obedience. Some may find it easy to laugh at these people and disregard their "authority." I do not. I weep for them because I know the inward pain and suffering that must be endured to live in such a contradiction.

Further, we may pray for such individuals that they will be filled with new power and authority. We may also become their friend and help in every way we can. If we will live out the cross-life before them, very soon we may discover that they are increasing in spiritual power and so are we.

9. THE DISCIPLINE OF SERVICE

Learn the lesson that, if you are to do the work of a prophet, what you need is not a scepter but a hoe.
—Bernard of Clairvaux

As the cross is the sign of submission, so the towel is the sign of service. When Jesus gathered His disciples for the Last Supper they were having trouble over who was the greatest. This was no new issue for them. "And an argument arose among them as to which of them was the greatest" (Lk. 9:46). Whenever there is trouble over who is the greatest there is trouble over who is the least. That is the crux of the matter for us, isn't it? Most of us know we will never be the greatest; just don't let us be the least.

Gathered at the Passover feast the disciples were keenly aware that someone needed to wash the others' feet. The problem was that the only people who washed feet were the least. So there they sat, feet caked with dirt. It was such a sore point that they were not even going to talk about it. No one wanted to be considered the least. Then Jesus took a towel and a basin and so redefined greatness.

Having lived out servanthood before them He called them to the way of service: "If I then, your Lord and Teacher, have washed your feet, you also ought to wash one another's feet. For I have given you an example, that you also should do as I have done to you" (Jn. 13:14, 15). In some ways we would prefer to hear Jesus' call to deny father and mother, houses and land for the sake of the gospel, than His word to wash feet. Radical self-denial gives the feel of adventure. If we forsake all, we even have the chance of glorious martyrdom. But in service we are banished to the mundane, the ordinary, the trivial.

In the Discipline of service there is also great liberty. Service en-

110

ables us to say "no!" to the world's games of promotion and authority. It abolishes our need (and desire) for a "pecking order." That phrase is so telling, so revealing. How like chickens we are! In the chicken pen there is no peace until it is clear who is the greatest and who is the least and who is at which rung everywhere in between. A group of people cannot be together for very long until the "pecking order" is clearly established. We can see it so easily in such things as where people sit, how they walk in relation to each other, who always gives way when two people are talking at the same time, who stands back when a job needs to be done and who steps forward. (Depending on the job it may be a sign of mastery or a sign of servitude.) These things are written on the face of human society.

The point is not that we are to do away with all sense of leadership or authority. Any sociologist would quickly demonstrate the impossibility of such a task. Even among Jesus and the disciples, leadership and authority are easily seen. The point is that Jesus completely redefined leadership and rearranged the lines of authority.

Jesus never taught that everyone had equal authority. In fact, He had a great deal to say about genuine spiritual authority and made it clear that many did not possess it. But the authority of which Jesus spoke is not the authority of a pecking order. We must clearly understand the radical nature of what Jesus taught on this matter. He was not just reversing the "pecking order," as many suppose. He was abolishing it. The authority of which He spoke was not an authority to manipulate and control. It was an authority of function, not of status.

Jesus declared, "You know that the rulers of the Gentiles lord it over them, and their great men exercise authority over them. *It shall not be so among you.*" He totally and completely rejected the pecking-order systems of His day. How then was it to be among them? "Whoever would be great among you must be your servant . . . even as the Son of man came not to be served but to serve" (Mt. 20:25–28). Therefore the spiritual authority of which Jesus spoke was an authority not found in a position or a title but in a towel.

Self-righteous Service vs. True Service

If true service is to be understood and practiced it must be distinguished clearly from "self-righteous service."

Self-righteous service comes through human effort. It expends immense amounts of energy calculating and scheming how to render the
service. Sociological charts and surveys may be devised so we can
"help those people." True service comes from a relationship with the
divine Other deep inside. We serve out of whispered promptings,
divine urgings. Energy is expended but it is not the frantic energy of
the flesh. Thomas Kelly writes, "I find He never guides us into an in-
tolerable scramble of panting feverishness." [1]

Self-righteous service is impressed with the "big deal." It is concerned to make impressive gains on ecclesiastical scoreboards. It
enjoys serving, especially when the service is titanic. True service
finds it almost impossible to distinguish the small from the large service. Where the difference is noted the true servant seems to be often
drawn to the small service, not out of false modesty, but because he
genuinely sees it as the important service. He indiscriminately wel-
comes all opportunities to serve.

Self-righteous service requires external rewards. It needs to know
that people see and appreciate the effort. It seeks human applause—
with proper religious modesty of course. True service rests contented
in hiddenness. It does not fear the lights and blare of attention, but it
does not seek them either. Since it is living out of a new Center of
Reference the divine nod of approval is completely sufficient.

Self-righteous service is highly concerned about results. It eagerly
waits to see if the person served will reciprocate in kind. It becomes
bitter when the results fall below expectations. True service is free of
the need to calculate results. It delights only in the service. It can
serve enemies as freely as friends.

Self-righteous service picks and chooses whom to serve. Sometimes
the high and powerful are served because that will insure a certain advantage. Sometimes the low and defenseless are served because that
will insure a humble image. True service is indiscriminate in its ministry. It has heard the command of Jesus to be the "servant of all" (Mk.
9:35). Brother Francis of Assisi wrote in a letter, "Being the servant
of all, I am bound to serve all and to administer the balm-bearing
words of my lord." [2]

Self-righteous service is affected by moods and whims. It can serve
only when there is a "feeling" to serve ("moved by the Spirit" as we
say). Ill health or inadequate sleep will control the desire to serve.

True service ministers simply and faithfully because there is a need. It knows that the "feeling to serve" can often be a hindrance to true service. It refuses to allow the feeling to control the service, but rather the service disciplines the feelings.

Self-righteous service is temporary. It functions only while the specific acts of service are being performed. Having served, it can rest easy. True service is a life-style. It acts from ingrained patterns of living. It springs spontaneously to meet human need.

Self-righteous service is without sensitivity. It insists on meeting the need even when to do so would be destructive. It demands the opportunity to help. True service can withhold the service as freely as perform it. It can listen with tenderness and patience before acting. It can serve by waiting in silence. "They also serve who only stand and wait."[3]

Self-righteous service fractures community. In the final analysis (once all the religious trappings are removed) it centers in the glorification of the individual. Therefore it puts others into our debt and becomes one of the most subtle and destructive forms of manipulation known. The result is the rupture of community.

True service, on the other hand, builds community. It quietly and unpretentiously goes about caring for the needs of others. It puts no one under obligation to return the service. It draws, binds, heals, builds. The result is the unity of the community.

Service and Humility

More than any other single way the grace of humility is worked into our lives through the Discipline of service. Humility, as we all know, is one of those virtues that is never gained by seeking it. The more we pursue it the more distant it becomes. To think we have it is sure evidence that we don't. Therefore most of us assume there is nothing we can do to gain this prized Christian virtue and so we do nothing.

But there *is* something we can do. We do not need to go through life faintly hoping that some day humility may fall upon our heads. Of all the classical Spiritual Disciplines, service is the most conducive to the growth of humility. When we set out on a consciously chosen course of action that accents the good of others and is for the most part a hidden work, a deep change occurs in our spirit.

Nothing *disciplines* the inordinate desires of the flesh like service, and nothing *transforms* the desires of the flesh like serving in hiddenness. The flesh whines against service but screams against hidden service. It strains and pulls for honor and recognition. It will devise subtle, religiously acceptable means to call attention to the service rendered. If we stoutly refuse to give in to this lust of the flesh we crucify it. Every time we crucify the flesh we crucify our pride and arrogance.

The apostle John wrote, "For all that is in the world, the lust of the flesh and the lust of the eyes and the pride of life, is not of the Father but is of the world" (1 Jn. 2:16). We fail to understand the force of this passage because of our tendency to relegate it all to sexual sin. The "lust of the flesh" refers to the failure to put under our control—to discipline—the natural human passions. C. H. Dodd has said that the "lust of the eyes" refers to "the tendency to be captivated by outward show." The "pride of life" he defines as "pretentious egoism." [4] In each case the same thing is seen: infatuation with natural human powers and abilities without any dependence upon God. That is the flesh in operation, and the flesh is the deadly enemy of humility.

The strictest daily discipline is necessary to hold these passions in check. The flesh must learn the painful lesson that it has no rights of its own. It is the work of hidden service that will accomplish this self-abasement.

William Law made a lasting impact upon eighteenth-century England with his book, *A Serious Call to a Devout and Holy Life*. In it Law urged that every day should be viewed as a day of humility. How do we go about making each day into a day of humility? By learning to serve others. Law understood that it was the Discipline of service that brings humility into the life. If we want humility he counsels us to

. . . condescend to all the weaknesses and infirmities of your fellow-creatures, cover their frailties, love their excellencies, encourage their virtues, relieve their wants, rejoice in their prosperities, compassionate their distress, receive their friendship, overlook their unkindness, forgive their malice, be a servant of servants, and condescend to do the lowest offices to the lowest of mankind. [5]

The result then of this daily discipline of the flesh will be the rise of the grace of humility. It will slip in upon us unawares. Though we do not sense its presence, we are aware of a fresh zest and exhilaration with living. We wonder at the new sense of confidence that marks our activities. Although the demands of life are as great as ever, we live in a new sense of unhurried peace. People whom we once only envied we now view with compassion, for we see not only their position but their pain. People whom we would have passed over we now see and find to be delightful individuals. We feel a new spirit of identification with the outcasts, the "offscourings" of the earth (1 Cor. 4:13).

Even more than the transformation that is occurring within us we are aware of a deeper love and joy in God. Our days are punctuated with spontaneous breathings of praise and adoration. Joyous hidden service to others is an acted prayer of thanksgiving. We seem to be directed by a new Control Center—and so we are.

Yes . . . But

A natural and understandable hesitancy accompanies any serious discussion of service. The hesitancy is good since it is wise to count the cost before plunging headlong into any Discipline. We experience a fear that comes out something like this: "If I do that, people will take advantage of me; they will walk all over me."

Right here we must see the difference between choosing to serve and choosing to be a servant. When we choose to serve we are still in charge. We decide whom we will serve and when we will serve. And if we are in charge we will worry a great deal about anyone's stepping on us, i.e., taking charge over us.

But when we choose to be a servant we give up the right to be in charge. There is a great freedom in this. If we voluntarily choose to be taken advantage of, then we cannot be manipulated. When we choose to be a servant we surrender the right to decide who and when we will serve. We become available and vulnerable.

Consider the perspective of a slave. A slave sees all of life from the viewpoint of slavery. He does not see himself as possessing the same rights as free men and women. Please understand me, when this slavery is involuntary it is cruel and dehumanizing.* When the slavery is

* A good part of my doctoral study was on slavery in America. I am keenly aware of the horribly demonic nature of involuntary servitude.

freely chosen, however, everything is changed. Voluntary servitude is a great joy.

The imagery of slavery may be difficult for us, but it was no trouble to the apostle Paul. He boasted frequently of his slavery to Christ, making lavish use of the first-century concept of the "love slave" (i.e., the slave who out of love has freely chosen to remain a slave). We do our best to soften Paul's language by translating the word "slave" as "servant." But whatever word we decide to use, let's be certain that we understand that Paul meant he had freely given up his rights.

Therefore the fear that we will be taken advantage of and stepped on is justified. That is exactly what may happen. But who can hurt some- one who has freely chosen to be stepped on? Thomas à Kempis in- structed us to be "so subject . . . that all men may go over thee and tread upon thee as upon mire of the street." [6]

A delightful story is told in *The Little Flowers of St. Francis* about how Francis taught Brother Leo the meaning of perfect joy. As the two walked together in the rain and bitter cold, Francis reminded Leo of all the things that the world—including the religious world— believed would bring joy, adding each time, "Perfect joy is not in that." Finally, in exasperation Brother Leo asked, "I beg you in God's name to tell me where perfect joy is." Whereupon Francis began enumerating the most humiliating self-abasing things he could imagine, adding each time, "Oh, Brother Leo, write that perfect joy is there." To explain and conclude the matter he told him, "Above all the graces and gifts of the Holy Spirit which Christ gives to His friends is that of conquering oneself and willingly enduring sufferings, insults, humiliations, and hardships for the love of Christ." [7]

We find those words hard to deal with today. (You must understand that I, too, struggle even to listen to the devotional masters on this point.) We fear that such an attitude will lead irrevocably down the path of excessive asceticism and self-mortification. In the church we are only now emerging from a "worm theology" that terribly de- valued human ability and potential. Does service lead back to that? No, certainly not. No doubt it is a danger we must always guard against. But we must also watch for the enemy in the opposite direc- tion. As Bonhoeffer said, "If there is no element of asceticism in our lives, if we give free rein to the desires of the flesh . . . we shall find it hard to train for the service of Christ." [8]

Service in the Marketplace

Service is not a list of things that we do, though in it we discover things to do. It is not a code of ethics but a way of living. To do specific acts of service is not the same thing as living in the Discipline of service. Just as there is more to the game of basketball than the rule book, there is more to service than specific acts of serving. It is one thing to *act* like a servant; it is quite another to *be* a servant. As in all the Disciplines, it is possible to master the mechanics of service without experiencing the Discipline.

To stress the inward nature of service, however, is not enough. Service to be service must take form and shape in the world in which we live. Therefore we must seek to perceive what service may look like in the marketplace of our daily lives.

At the outset there is the service of hiddenness. Even public leaders can cultivate tasks of service that remain generally unknown. If all of our serving is before others we will be shallow people indeed. Listen to the spiritual direction of Jeremy Taylor: "Love to be concealed, and little esteemed: be content to want [lack] praise, never be troubled when thou art slighted or undervalued . . . ." [9] Hiddenness is a rebuke to the flesh and can deal a fatal blow to pride.

At first thought it would seem that hidden service is only for the sake of the individual served. Such is not the case. Hidden anonymous ministries affect even people who know nothing of them. They sense a deeper love and compassion among people, though they cannot account for the feeling. If a secret service is done on their behalf they are inspired to deeper devotion, for they know that the well of service is far deeper than they can see. It is a ministry that can frequently be engaged in by all people. It sends ripples of joy and celebration in any community of people.

There is the service of small things. Like Dorcas, we find ways to make "coats and garments for the widows" (Acts 9:39). The following is a true story. As I was in the frantic final throes of writing my doctoral dissertation I received a phone call from a friend. His wife had taken the car and he wondered if I could take him on a number of errands. Trapped, I consented, inwardly cursing my luck. As I ran out the door I grabbed Bonhoeffer's *Life Together,* thinking that I might have an opportunity to read in it. Through each errand I inwardly fretted and fumed at the loss of precious time. Finally, at a supermarket, the final stop, I waved my friend on saying I would wait in the car. I picked up my book, opened it to the marker and read these words:

> The second service that one should perform for another in a Christian community is that of active helpfulness. This means, initially, simple assistance in trifling, external matters. There is a multitude of these things wherever people live together. Nobody is too good for the meanest service. One who worries about the loss of time that such petty, outward acts of helpfulness entail is usually taking the importance of his own career too solemnly.[10]

Francis de Sales says that the great virtues and the small fidelities are like sugar and salt. Sugar may have a more exquisite taste but its use is less frequent. Salt is found everywhere. The great virtues are a rare occurrence; the ministry of small things is a daily service. Large tasks require great sacrifice for a moment; small things require constant sacrifice. "The small occasions . . . return every moment . . . . If we want to be faithful to these small things, nature never has time to breathe, and we must die to all our inclinations. We should a hundred times rather make some great sacrifices to God, however violent and painful, on condition that we be freed with liberty to follow our tastes and habits in every little detail."[11]

In the realm of the spirit we soon discover that the real issues are found in the tiny insignificant corners of life. Our infatuation with the "big deal" has blinded us to this fact. The service of small things will put us at odds with our sloth and idleness. We will come to see small things as the central issues. Fénelon said: "It is not elevation of the spirit to feel contempt for small things. It is, on the contrary, because of too narrow points of view that we consider as little what has such far reaching consequences."[12]

There is the service of guarding the reputation of others. Or as Bernard of Clairvaux put it, the service of "Charity." How necessary this is if we are to be saved from backbiting and gossip. The apostle Paul taught us to "speak evil of no one" (Tit. 3:2). We may clothe our backbiting in all the religious respectability we want but it will remain a deadly poison. There is a discipline in holding one's tongue that can work wonders in our inward person.

Nor should we be a party to the slanderous talk of others. We have a rule on the pastoral team of our church which our people have come to appreciate. We refuse to allow any member of the congregation to speak disparagingly of one pastor to another pastor. Gently but firmly we ask them to go directly to the offending pastor. Eventually people understand that we simply will not allow them to talk to us about pastor so-and-so. This rule, held to by our entire team, has had beneficial results.

Bernard warned us that the spiteful tongue "strikes a deadly blow at charity in all who hear him speak and, so far as it can, destroys root and branch, not only in the immediate hearers but also in all others to whom the slander, flying from lip to lip, is afterwards repeated." [13] Guarding the reputation of others is a deep and lasting service.

There is the service of being served. When Jesus began to wash the feet of those He loved, Peter refused. He would never let his Master stoop to such a menial service on his behalf. It sounds like a statement of humility; in reality it was an act of veiled pride. Jesus' service was an affront to Peter's concept of authority. If Peter had been the master he would not have washed feet!

It is an act of submission and service to allow others to serve us. It recognizes their "kingdom authority" over us. We graciously receive the service rendered, never feeling we must repay it. Those who out of pride refuse to be served are failing to submit to the divinely appointed leadership in the kingdom of God.

There is the service of common courtesy. Such deeds of compassion have fallen on hard times in our day. But we who are of the light must never despise the rituals of relationship that are in every culture. It is one of the few ways left in modern society of acknowledging the value of one another. As Paul counseled Titus, we are " to be gentle, and to show perfect courtesy toward all men" (Tit. 3:2).

Missionaries understand the value of courtesy. They would not dare to come blundering into some village demanding to be heard without first going through the appropriate rituals of introduction and acquaintanceship. Yet we feel we can violate these rituals in our own culture and still be received and heard. And we wonder why no one will listen.

"But they are so meaningless, so hypocritical," we complain. That is a myth. They are extremely meaningful and not in the least hypocritical. Once we get over our egocentric arrogance about the fact that people don't really want to know how we are when they say "How are you?'' we can see that it is just an American way of acknowledging our presence. We can wave and acknowledge their presence too without feeling the need to give a prognosis on our latest headache. Words of "thank you" and "yes, please,'' letters of appreciation and RSVP responses are all services of courtesy. The specific acts will vary from culture to culture but the purpose is always the same: to acknowledge others and affirm their worth. The service of courtesy is sorely needed in our increasingly computerized and depersonalized society.

There is the service of hospitality. Peter urges us to "practice hospitality ungrudgingly to one another" (1 Pet. 4:9). Paul does the same and even makes it one of the requirements for the office of bishop (Rom. 12:13; 1 Tim. 3:2; Tit. 1:8). There is a desperate need today for homes that can be open to one another. The old idea of the guest house has been made obsolete by the proliferation of modern motels and restaurants, but we may seriously question whether the change is an advance. I have walked through the Spanish missions of California and marveled at the gracious and adequate provision that was made for visitors. Perhaps it is the modern shiny depersonalized motels that should be obsolete.

I know of a couple who have sought to make the ministry of hospitality a priority in their lives. In any given month they may have as many as seventy individuals come to their home. It is a service to which they believe God has called them. Perhaps most of us cannot do that much but we can do something. We can begin somewhere.

Sometimes we limit ourselves because we make hospitality too complicated. I remember an occasion where the hostess was scurrying around with this and that, sincerely wanting to make everyone feel comfortable. My friend startled us all (and put everyone at ease) by saying, "Helen, I don't want any coffee, I don't want any tea, I don't want any cookies, I don't want a napkin, I just want to visit. Won't you sit down and talk with us!" Just a chance to be together and share—that is the stuff of hospitality.

There is the service of listening. "The first service that one owes to others in the fellowship consists in listening to them. Just as love to God begins with listening to His Word, so the beginning of love for the brethren is learning to listen to them." [14] We need so desperately the help that can come through listening to one another. We do not need to be trained psychoanalysts to be trained listeners. The most important requirements are compassion and patience.

We do not have to have the correct answers to listen well. In fact, often the correct answers are a hindrance to listening for we become more anxious to give the answer than to hear. An impatient half-listening is an affront to the person sharing.

To listen to others quiets and disciplines the mind to listen to God. It creates an inward working upon the heart that transforms the affections, even the priorities, of the life. When we have grown dull in listening to God we would do well to listen to others in silence and see if we do not hear God. "Anyone who thinks that his time is too valuable to spend keeping quiet will eventually have no time for God and his brother, but only for himself and for his own follies." [15]

There is the service of bearing the burdens of each other. "Bear one another's burdens, and so fulfill the law of Christ" (Gal. 6:2). The "law of Christ" is the law of love, the "royal law" as James called it (Jas. 2:8). Love is most perfectly fulfilled when we bear the hurts and sufferings of each other, weeping with those who weep.

If we care we will learn to bear their sorrows. I say "learn" because this, too, is a discipline to be mastered. Most of us too easily assume that all we need to do is decide to bear the burdens of others and we can do it. Then we try it for a time and soon the joy of life has left and we are heavy with the sorrows of others. It does not need to be so. We can learn to uphold the burdens of others without ourselves being destroyed by them. Jesus, who bore the burdens of the whole world, could say, "My yoke is easy, and my burden is light" (Mt. 11:30) Can we learn to lift the sorrows and pains of others into the tender arms of Jesus so that our burden is lighter? Of course we can. But it takes some practice, so rather than dashing out to bear the burdens of the whole world, let's begin more humbly. Begin in some small corner somewhere and learn. Jesus will be your Teacher.

Finally, there is the service of sharing the word of Life with one another. The Poustinias that were established by Catherine Doherty had a rule: those who went into the deserts of silence and solitude did so for others. Any word that they received from God they were to bring back and share with others. This is a gracious service to be rendered, for no individual can hear all that God wants to say. We are dependent upon one another to receive the full counsel of God. The smallest member can bring us a word—we dare not despise the service.

It is, of course, a fearful thing to proclaim these words to each other. Often there is mixture: "from the same mouth come blessing and cursing" (Jas. 3:10). Such realities humble us and throw us in deep dependence upon God. But we must not draw back from this service for it is desperately needed today.

Service that is duty-motivated breathes death. Service that flows out of our inward person is life, and joy and peace. The risen Christ beckons us to the ministry of the towel. Perhaps you would like to begin by experimenting with a prayer that a number of us have used. Begin the day by praying, "Lord Jesus, I would so appreciate it if You would bring me someone today whom I can serve."

PART III
The Corporate Disciplines

10. THE DISCIPLINE OF CONFESSION

The confession of evil works is the first beginning of good works.—Augustine of Hippo

At the heart of God is the desire to forgive and to give. Because of this He set into motion the entire redemptive process that culminated in the cross and was confirmed in the resurrection. The usual notion of what Jesus did on the cross runs something like this: people were so bad and so mean and God was so angry with them that He would not forgive them unless somebody big enough could take the rap for the whole lot of them.

Nothing could be further from the truth. Love, not anger, brought Jesus to the cross. Golgotha came as a result of God's great desire to forgive, not His reluctance. Jesus saw that by His vicarious suffering He could actually internalize all the evil of mankind and so heal it, forgive it.

That is why Jesus refused the customary painkiller when it was offered Him. He wanted to be completely alert for this greatest work of redemption. In a deep and mysterious way He was preparing to enter the collective unconscious of the human race. Since Jesus lives in the Eternal Now, this work was not just for those around Him, but He was taking in all the violence, all the fear, all the sin of all the past, all the present, and all the future. This was His highest and most holy work, the work which makes confession and the forgiveness of sins possible.

Some seem to think that when Jesus shouted "My God, my God, why hast Thou forsaken me?" it was a moment of weakness (Mk. 15:34). Not at all. *This was His moment of greatest triumph.* Jesus, who had walked in constant communion with the Father, now became so totally identified with mankind that He was the actual embodiment of sin. As Paul wrote, ''he made him to be sin who knew no sin'' (2 Cor. 5:21). Jesus had succeeded in taking into Himself all the dark powers of this present evil age and had defeated every one of them by the light of His presence. He had accomplished such a total identification with the sin of the race that He sensed the abandonment of God. Only in that way could He redeem sin. It was indeed His moment of greatest triumph.

Having accomplished this greatest of all His works, Jesus then took refreshment. ''It is finished,'' He said. That is, this work of redemption was completed. He could feel the last dregs of the misery of mankind flow through Him and into the care of the Father. The last twinges of evil, hostility, anger and fear drained out of Him and He was able to turn again into the light of God's presence. ''It is finished.'' The task is complete. Soon after, He was free to give up His spirit to the Father.

> To shame our sins He blushed in blood;
> He closed His eyes to show us God;
> Let all the world fall down and know
> That none but God such love can show.
> —Bernard of Clairvaux

This redemptive process is a great mystery hidden in the heart of God. But I know that it is true. I know this not only because the Bible says it is true but because I have seen its effects in the lives of many people, including myself. It is the ground upon which we can know that confession and forgiveness are realities that transform us. Without the cross the Discipline of confession would be only psychologically therapeutic. But it is so much more. It involves an objective change in our relationship with God and a subjective change in us. It is a means of healing and transforming the inner spirit.

''But I thought that Christ on the cross and redemption had to do with salvation,'' you may say. It does. But salvation as the Bible speaks of it refers to far more than who will get to heaven or who will become a Christian. To converted people Paul said, ''Work out your own salvation with fear and trembling'' (Phil. 2:12). In a sermon titled ''The Repentance of Believers,'' John Wesley spoke of the necessity of Christians to come into more of the forgiving grace of God. The Discipline of confession can help the believer to grow into "mature manhood, to the measure of the stature of the fullness of Christ" (Eph. 4:13).

"But isn't confession a grace instead of a Discipline?" It is both. Unless God gives the grace, no genuine confession can be made. But it is also a Discipline because there are things we must do. It is a consciously chosen course of action that brings us under the shadow of the Almighty.

"How is it that confession is listed under the Corporate Disciplines? I thought this was a private matter between the individual and God." Again the answer is not "either/or" but "both/and." We are grateful for the biblical teaching, underscored in the Reformation, that "there is one mediator between God and men, the man Christ Jesus" (1 Tim. 2:5). We are also grateful for the biblical teaching, newly appreciated in our day, to "confess your sins to one another, and pray for one another . . ." (Jas. 5:16). Both are found in Scripture and neither needs to exclude the other.

Confession is so difficult a Discipline for us partly because we view the believing community as a fellowship of saints before we see it as a fellowship of sinners. We come to feel that everyone else has advanced so far into holiness that we are isolated and alone in our sin. We could not bear to reveal our failures and shortcomings to others. We imagine that we are the only ones who have not stepped onto the high road to heaven. Therefore we hide ourselves from one another and live in veiled lies and hypocrisy.

But if we know that the people of God are first a fellowship of sinners we are freed to hear the unconditional call of God's love and to confess our need openly before our brothers and sisters. We know we are not alone in our sin. The fear and pride which cling to us like barnacles cling to others also. We are sinners together. In acts of mutual confession we release the power that heals. Our humanity is no longer denied but transformed.

Authority to Forgive

The followers of Jesus Christ have been given the authority to receive the confession of sin and to forgive it in His name. "If you forgive the

sins of any, they are forgiven; if you retain the sins of any, they are retained'' (Jn. 20:23). What a wonderful privilege! Why do we shy
away from such a life-giving ministry? If we, not out of merit but
sheer grace, have been given the authority to set others free, how dare
we withhold this great gift? ''Our brother . . . has been given to us to
help us. He hears the confession of our sins in Christ's stead and he
forgives our sins in Christ's name. He keeps the secret of our confession as God keeps it. When I go to my brother to confess, I am going
to God.'' [1]

Such authority in no way threatens the value or efficacy of private
confession. It is a wonderful truth that the individual can break
through into new life in the cross without the aid of any human mediator. That reality swept like a breath of fresh air in the days of the Reformation. It became a trumpet call of liberation from the bondage and
manipulation that had crept into the ecclesiastical confessional system.
But we also need to remember that Luther himself believed in mutual,
brotherly confession. In the Large Catechism he wrote, ''Therefore
when I admonish you to confession I am admonishing you to be a
Christian.'' [2] Nor should we forget that when the confessional system
was first introduced into the church it sparked a genuine revival of personal piety and holiness.

The individual who has known through private confession the forgiveness and the release from persistent nagging habits of sin should
rejoice greatly in this evidence of God's mercy. But there are others
for whom that has not happened. Let me describe what it is like. We
have prayed, even begged, for forgiveness, and though we hope we
have been forgiven we have sensed no release. We have doubted our
forgiveness and despaired at our confession. We have feared that
perhaps we had made confession only to ourselves and not to God.
The haunting sorrows and hurts of the past have not been healed. We
had tried to convince ourselves that God only forgives the sin, He does
not heal the memory, but deep within we know there must be something more. People have told us to take our forgiveness by faith and
not to call God a liar. Not wanting to call God a liar, we do our best to
take it by faith. But because misery and bitterness remain in our life
we again despair. Eventually we begin to believe either that forgiveness is only a ticket to heaven and not meant to affect our lives now,
or that we are not worthy of the forgiving grace of God.

Those of us who in some small way identify with these words can rejoice. We have not exhausted our resources nor God's grace when we have tried private confession. In the Book of Common Prayer we read these encouraging words following the call to self-examination and repentance: "If there be any of you who by this means cannot quiet his own conscience herein but require further comfort or counsel, let him come to me or to some other minister of God's word, and open his grief. . . ."[3] God has given us our brothers and sisters to stand in Christ's stead and make God's presence and forgiveness real to us.

The Scripture teaches us that all believers are priests before God. "You are a chosen race, a royal priesthood" (1 Pet. 2:9). At the time of the Reformation this was called "the universal priesthood of all believers." One of the functions of the Old Testament priest was to bring the forgiveness of sins through the holy sacrifice. The book of Hebrews, of course, makes clear that Jesus is the final and sufficient sacrifice. But He has given to us His priesthood, the ministry of making that sacrifice real in the hearts and lives of other human beings. It is through the voice of our brothers and sisters that the word of forgiveness is heard and takes root in our lives. Bonhoeffer wrote: "A man who confesses his sins in the presence of a brother knows that he is no longer alone with himself; he experiences the presence of God in the reality of the other person. As long as I am by myself in the confession of my sins everything remains in the dark, but in the presence of a brother the sin has to be brought into the light."[4]

The stylized form of this avenue of help has been called the Confessional or the sacrament of penance. Though many of us, myself included, would feel highly uncomfortable with that form of confession, it does have certain advantages. First, the formalized form of the printed confession does not allow for any excuses or extenuating circumstances. The individual must confess that he has sinned by his own fault, his own most grievous fault. One's sins cannot be called errors in judgment, nor is there any room to blame them on upbringing, or family, or mean neighbors. This is a Reality Therapy of the best sort since we are so prone to blame our sins on everybody and everything before we will take personal responsibility for them.

A second advantage of the confessional is that the word of forgiveness is expected and given in the absolution. The word of Scripture, or some similar word, is actually spoken out loud. "If we confess our sins, he is faithful and just, and will forgive our sins and cleanse us from all unrighteousness" (1 Jn. 1:9). The penitent is then told in clear authoritative words that he is totally forgiven and set free of his sin. The assurance of forgiveness is sealed in the spirit when it is spoken by our brother or sister in the name of Christ.

There is a third advantage to the institutionalized Confessional, namely penance. If penance is viewed as a way of earning forgiveness, it is dangerous indeed. But if it is seen as an opportunity to pause a moment to consider the seriousness of our sin, then it has genuine merit. Today we take far too lightly our offenses to the love of God. If we had only a tinge of the sense of revulsion that God feels toward sin, we would be moved to holier living. God pleads with us, "Oh, do not do this abominable thing that I‧ hate!" (Jer. 44:4). The purpose of penance is to help us move into that deeper sense of the sinfulness of sin.

These things can, of course, be accomplished without a formalized Confessional. In fact, when we know what we are about, it is an enormous advance to see the ministry of confession as the common property of the people of God. How can this be done? Perhaps a living example will aid in making these concepts more concrete.

Diary of a Confession

Although I had read in the Bible about the ministry of confession in the Christian brotherhood, I had never experienced it until I was pastoring my first church.

I did not take the difficult step of laying bare my inner life to another out of any deep burden or sense of sin. I did not feel there was anything wrong in the least—except one thing. I longed for more power to do the work of God. I felt inadequate for many of the desperate needs with which I was confronted. There had to be more spiritual resources than I was experiencing (and I'd had all the Holy Spirit experiences you're supposed to have—you name them, I'd had them!). "Lord, is there more You want to bring into my life?" I prayed. "I want to be conquered and ruled by You. If there is any block in my life for the flow of Your power, reveal it to me." He did. Not by an audible voice or even through any human voice but simply by a growing impression that perhaps something in my past was impeding the flow of His life. So I devised a plan. I divided my life into three periods: childhood, adolescence, adulthood. On the first day I came before God in prayer and meditation, pencil and paper in hand. Inviting Him to reveal to me anything during my childhood that needed either forgiveness or healing or both, I waited in absolute silence for some ten minutes. Anything about my childhood that surfaced to my conscious mind I wrote down. I made no attempt to analyze the items or put any value judgment on them. My assurance was that God would reveal anything that needed His healing touch. Having finished, I set the paper down for the day. The next day I went through the same exercise for my adolescent years, and the third day for my adult years.

Paper in hand I then went to a dear brother in Christ. I had informed him a week ahead, so he understood the purpose of our meeting. Slowly, sometimes painfully, I read my sheet adding only those comments necessary to make the sin clear. When I had finished, I began to return the paper to my briefcase. Wisely, my counselor-confessor gently stopped my hand and took the sheet of paper. Without a word he took a wastebasket, and as I watched he tore the paper into hundreds of tiny pieces and dropped them into the basket. That powerful nonverbal expression of forgiveness was followed by a simple absolution. My sins I knew were as far away as the East is from the West.

Next my friend, with the laying on of hands, prayed a prayer of healing for all of the sorrows and hurts of the past. The power of that prayer lives with me today.

I cannot say I experienced any dramatic feelings. I did not. In fact, the entire experience was an act of sheer obedience with no compelling feelings in the least. But I am convinced that it set me free in ways I had not known before. It seemed that I was released to explore what was for me new and uncharted regions of the Spirit. Following that event I began to move into several of the Disciplines described in this book that I had never experienced before. Was there a causal connection? I do not know and frankly I do not care. It is enough to have obeyed the inner prompting from above.

There was one interesting sidelight. The exposure of my humanity evidently sparked a freedom in my counselor-friend, for directly following his prayer for me he was able to express a deep and troubling sin that he had been unable to confess until then. Freedom begets freedom.

Counsel in the Giving of a Confession

Not only is it true that "we love, because He first loved us" but we are enabled to make confession only and especially because He first loved us (1 John 4:19). The evidence of mercy and grace sparks a contrite heart and allows confession to flow. We are drawn to Him as Hosea tells us "with cords of compassion, with the bands of love" (Hos. 11:4). We come with hopeful hearts, for the One we are coming to waits for us like the father of the prodigal who saw his son when he was still a great way off and in compassion ran and embraced him and welcomed him back (Lk. 15:20). His greatest delight is to forgive. He calls His light-filled creatures of heaven into celebration whenever one person makes confession.

What do we do? St. Alphonsus Luguori writes, "For a good confession three things are necessary: an examination of conscience, sorrow, and a determination to avoid sin."[5]

"An examination of conscience." This is a time, as Douglas Steere has said, "where a soul comes under the gaze of God and where in His silent and loving Presence this soul is pierced to the quick and becomes conscious of the things that must be forgiven and put right before it can continue to love One whose care has been so constant."[6]

In this experience of opening ourselves to the "gaze of God," we must be prepared to deal with definite sins. A generalized confession may save us from humiliation and shame but it will not ignite inward healing. The people who came to Jesus came with obvious, specific sins, and they were forgiven each one. It is far too easy to avoid our real guilt in a general confession. In our confession we bring concrete sins. By calling them concrete, however, I do not mean only outward sins. I mean definite sins, the sins of the heart: pride, avarice, anger, fear, as well as the sins of the flesh: sloth, gluttony, lust, murder. We may use the method described earlier. Perhaps we will be drawn to the method Luther used, in which he sought to examine himself on the basis of the Ten Commandments. We may be led to another approach altogether.

In our desire to be specific we must not, however, run to the opposite danger of being unduly concerned to rout out every last detail in our lives. With profound common sense Francis de Sales counseled, "Do not feel worried if you do not remember all your little peccadilloes in confession, for as you often fall imperceptibly, so you are often raised up imperceptibly." [7]

"Sorrow" is necessary to a good confession. Sorrow as it relates to confession is not primarily an emotion, though emotion may be involved. It is an abhorrence at having committed the sin, a deep regret at having offended the heart of the Father. Sorrow is an issue of the will before it is an issue of the emotions. In fact, being sorrowful in the emotions without a godly sorrow in the will destroys the confession.

Sorrow is a way of taking the confession seriously. It is the opposite of the priest, and undoubtedly the penitent, ridiculed by Chaucer in *The Canterbury Tales:*

> Full sweetly heard he confession,
> And pleasant was his absolution. [8]

"A determination to avoid sin" is the third essential for a good confession. In the Discipline of confession we ask God to give us a yearning for holy living, a hatred for unholy living. John Wesley once said: "Give me one hundred preachers who fear nothing but sin and desire nothing but God . . . such alone will shake the gates of hell and set up the kingdom of heaven on earth." [9] It is the *will* to be delivered from sin that we seek from God as we prepare to make confession. We must desire to be conquered and ruled by God, or if we do not desire it, to desire to desire it. Such a desire is a gracious gift from God. The seeking of this gift is one of the preliminaries for confessing to a brother or sister.

Does all this sound complicated? Do you fear you might miss one of the points and thus render everything ineffectual? It is usually much more complicated in the analysis than in the experience. Remember the heart of the Father; He is like a shepherd who will risk anything to find that one lost sheep. We do not have to make God willing to forgive. In fact, it is God who is working to make us willing to seek His forgiveness.

One further note on the preparation for confession. There must be a definite termination point in the self-examination process. Otherwise we can easily fall into a permanent habit of self-condemnation. Confession begins in sorrow but it ends in joy. There is celebration in the forgiveness of sins because it results in a genuinely changed life.

Then there is the practical matter of to whom we should go to confess. It is quite correct theologically to say that every Christian believer can receive the confession of another. But not every Christian believer will have sufficient empathy and understanding. Though it is unfortunate, it is a fact of life that some individuals seem unable to keep a confidence. Others would be disqualified because they would be horrified at the revealing of certain sins. Still others, not understanding the nature and value of confession, would try to shrug it off with a "That's not so bad." Fortunately many people do understand and would be delighted to minister in this way. These people are found by asking God to reveal them to us. Even the discovery of to whom we should confess can be a gracious exercise of the Discipline of prayer.

But what if there is an offense we could never bring ourselves to reveal? What if we lack the courage to open a particular corner of our lives? Then all we need to do is say to our brother or sister: "I need your help. There is a sin which I cannot bring myself to confess." Our confessor-friend will "then adopt an easy means of dragging from its den the wild beast that would devour you. All you will have to do is to answer Yes or Nor to his interrogations. And behold, both the temporal and the eternal hell have disappeared, the grace of God is recovered, and peace of conscience reigns supreme." [10]

Counsel in the Receiving of a Confession

Like any spiritual ministry there is a preparation involved in being able to hear rightly the confession of a brother or sister.

We begin by learning to live under the cross. Bonhoeffer said: "Anybody who lives beneath the Cross and who has discerned in the Cross of Jesus the utter wickedness of all men and of his own heart will find there is no sin that can ever be alien to him. Anybody who has once been horrified by the dreadfulness of his own sin that nailed Jesus to the Cross will no longer be horrified by even the rankest sins of a brother.'' [11] This is the one thing that will save us from ever being offended in the confession of another. It forever delivers us from conveying any attitude of superiority. We know the deceptiveness of the human heart and we know the grace and mercy of God's acceptance. Once we see the awfulness of sin we know that regardless of what others have done we ourselves are the chief of sinners.

Therefore there is nothing that anyone could say that would disturb us. Nothing. By living under the cross we can hear the worst possible things from the best possible people without so much as batting an eye. If we live in that reality we will convey that spirit to others. They know it is safe to come to us. They know we can receive anything they could possibly reveal. They know we would never condescend to them but instead understand.

When we live in this spirit we do not need to tell others that we will keep privileged information privileged. They know we would never betray a confidence. We do not have to tell them. Nor would we ever be tempted to betray it, for we know the godly sorrow that has driven them to this difficult step.

By living under the cross we are delivered from the danger of spiritual domination. We have stood where our brother now stands and so the desire to use his confession against him is gone. Nor do we feel any need to control him or to straighten him out. All we feel is acceptance and understanding.

As we prepare for this sacred ministry it is wise that we regularly pray for an increase of the light of Christ within us, so that as we are with others we will radiate His life and light into them. We want to learn how to live so that our very presence will speak of the love and forgiving grace of God. Also we should pray for an increase of the gift of discernment. That is especially important when after the confession we pray for them. We need to be able to perceive the real healing needed in the deep inner spirit.

It is important that when others are opening their griefs to us we discipline ourselves to be quiet. We will be severely tempted to relieve the tension of the situation by some offhanded comment. This is very distracting and even destructive to the sacredness of the moment. Neither should we try to pry out more details than are necessary. If we feel that out of embarrassment or fear they are holding something back, the best method is to wait silently and prayerfully.

On one occasion an individual was confessing her sorrow to me and to the Lord. When she finished I felt impressed to wait in silence. Presently she began sharing a deep inward sin that she had never been able to tell anyone. Later she told me that as I waited she looked at me and "saw" superimposed upon my eyes the eyes of Another which conveyed to her a love and acceptance that released her to unburden her heart. I had felt nothing nor did I "see" anything but I do not doubt her experience for it did result in a wonderful inner healing.

That story illustrates another important factor in receiving a confession. It is often helpful to set the cross between yourself and the penitent.* This is done by prayer through the imagination. This protects them from receiving from you merely human emotion and protects you from receiving from them any harmful influences. Everything is filtered through the light of the cross. Your human compassion is heightened and enlivened by divine love. You are praying for them through the power of the cross.

It hardly needs to be said that as they share you are praying for them. Inwardly and imperceptively (it would be unkind to make a display of your praying) you are beaming prayers of love and forgiveness into them. Also you are praying that they will share the "key" that would reveal any area needing the healing touch of Christ.

Finally, it is extremely important that you pray for the person and not just counsel with them. Before or during the prayer we should announce to them that the forgiveness that is in Jesus Christ is now real and effective for them. We can say this in words and tones of genuine authority for we have all of heaven behind the absolution (Jn. 20:22, 23).†

The prayer is for the healing of the inner wounds that the sin has caused. It is best to accompany the prayer with the "laying on of

---

* This advice, and much more, was given to me by Agnes Sanford. I have discovered her to be an extremely wise and skillful counselor in these matters. Her book *The Healing Gifts of the Spirit* is an excellent resource.

† In these words of Jesus we have not only the ministry of forgiving sins but the ministry of retaining sins. "If you forgive the sins of any, they are forgiven; if you retain the sins of any, they are retained." The ministry of retaining sins is simply the refusal to try to bring people into something for which they are not ready. Sometimes people are so anxious to get others into the kingdom that they will try to announce their forgiveness before they have sought it or even wanted it. Unfortunately this malady is characteristic of a great deal of modern evangelism.

hands'' which is an elemental teaching of the Bible and is a means through which God communicates His life-giving power (Heb. 6:2). Invite God to flow into the deep inner mind and heal the sorrows of the past. Picture the healing. Thank Him for it. Of this ministry of prayer Agnes Sanford writes:

> One makes a very deep rapport in this kind of prayer. One feels the feelings of the person for whom one prays; so much so that often the tears come from some deep center of compassion within the soul. Yet, if one weeps, it is not in grief but in joy, knowing that these tears are not one's own but are the tears of the compassionate heart of Christ brooding over this lost one, and the joy of Christ that at last He has been given a channel through which He can reach this person whom He loves.[12]

The Discipline of confession brings an end to pretense. God is calling into being a church that can openly confess its frail humanity and know the forgiving and empowering graces of Christ. Honesty leads to confession, and confession leads to change. May God give grace to the church once again to recover the Discipline of confession.

11. THE DISCIPLINE OF WORSHIP

To worship is to quicken the conscience by the holiness of God, to feed the mind with the truth of God, to purge the imagination by the beauty of God, to open the heart to the love of God, to devote the will to the purpose of God.
—*William Temple*

To worship is to experience reality, to touch Life. It is to know, to feel, to experience the resurrected Christ in the midst of the gathered community. It is a breaking into the Shekinah* of God, or better yet, being invaded by the Shekinah of God.

God is actively seeking worshipers. Jesus declared, "The true worshipers will worship the Father in spirit and truth, for such the Father *seeks* to worship him" (Jn. 4:23). It is God who seeks, draws, persuades. Worship is human response to divine initiative. In Genesis God walked in the garden seeking out Adam and Eve. In the crucifixion Jesus drew men and women to himself (Jn. 12:32). Scripture is replete with examples of God's efforts to initiate, restore, and maintain fellowship with His children. God is like the father of the prodigal who, seeing his son a long way off, rushed to welcome him home.

Worship is our responding to the overtures of love from the heart of the Father. Its central reality is found "in spirit and truth." It is kindled within us only when the Spirit of God touches our human spirit. Forms and rituals do not produce worship, nor does the formal disuse of forms and rituals. We can use all the right techniques and methods, we can have the best possible liturgy, but we have not worshiped the Lord until Spirit touches spirit. The words of the chorus, "Set my spirit free that I may worship Thee," reveal the basis

---

* The glory or the radiance of God dwelling in the midst of His people. It denotes the immediate Presence of God as opposed to a God who is abstract or aloof.

of worship. Until God touches and frees our spirit we cannot enter this realm. Singing, praying, praising all may lead to worship, but worship is more than any of them. Our spirit must be ignited by divine fire.

As a result we can be indifferent to the question of a correct form for worship. The issue of high liturgy or low liturgy, this form or that form, is peripheral rather than central. We are encouraged in our indifference when we realize that nowhere does the New Testament prescribe a particular form for worship. In fact, what we find is a freedom that is incredible for people with such deep roots in the synagogue liturgical system. They had the reality. When Spirit touched spirit, forms became irrelevant.

The Object of Our Worship

Jesus answered for all time the question of whom we are to worship. "You shall worship the Lord your God and him only shall you serve" (Mt. 4:10). The one true God is the God of Abraham, Isaac, and Jacob; the God whom Jesus Christ revealed. God made clear His hatred for all idolatries by placing an incisive command at the start of the Decalogue. "You shall have no other gods before me" (Ex. 20:3). Nor does idolatry consist only in bowing before visible objects of adoration. A. W. Tozer says, "The essence of idolatry is the entertainment of thoughts about God that are unworthy of Him." [1] To think rightly about God is in an important sense to have everything right. To think wrongly about God is in an important sense to have everything wrong.

We desperately need to see who God is: to read about His self-disclosure to His ancient people Israel, to meditate on His attributes, to gaze upon the revelation of His nature in Jesus Christ. When we see the Lord of hosts "high and lifted up," ponder His infinite wisdom and knowledge, wonder at His unfathomable mercy and love, we cannot help but move into doxology.

> Glad thine attributes confess,
> Glorious all and numberless. [2]

To see who the Lord is brings us to confession. When Isaiah caught sight of the glory of God he cried, "Woe is me! For I am lost; for I am a man of unclean lips, and I dwell in the midst of a people of unclean lips; for my eyes have seen the King, the Lord of hosts!'' (Is. 6:5). The pervasive sinfulness of human beings becomes evident when contrasted with the radiant holiness of God. Our fickleness becomes extreme once we see God's faithfulness. To understand His grace is to understand our guilt.

We worship the Lord not only because of who He is but also because of what He has done. Above all, the God of the Bible is the God who acts. His goodness, faithfulness, justice, mercy all can be seen in His dealings with His people. His gracious actions are not only etched into ancient history, but are engraved into our personal histories. As the apostle Paul said, the only reasonable response is worship (Rom. 12:1). We praise God for who He is, and thank Him for what He has done.

The Priority of Worship

If the Lord is to be *Lord,* worship must have priority in our lives. The *first* commandment of Jesus is ''Love the Lord your God with all your heart, and with all your soul, and with all your mind, and with all your strength'' (Mk. 12:30). The divine priority is worship first, service second. Our lives are to be punctuated with praise, thanksgiving and adoration. Service flows out of worship. Service as a substitute for worship is idolatry. Activity may become the enemy of adoration.

God declared that the primary function of the Levitical priests was to ''come near to me to minister to me'' (Ezek. 44:15). For the Old Testament priesthood, ministry to Him was to precede all other work. And that is no less true of the universal priesthood of the New Testament. One grave temptation we all face is to run around answering calls to service without ministering to the Lord himself.

Preparation for Worship

A striking features of worship in the Bible is that people gathered in what we could call only a ''holy expectancy.'' They believed they would actually hear the *Kol Yahweh,* the voice of God. When Moses went into the Tabernacle he knew he was entering the Presence of God. The same was true of the early church. It was not surprising to them that the building in which they met shook with the power of God. It had happened before (Acts 2:2; 4:31). When some dropped dead and others were raised from the dead by the word of the Lord the people knew that God was in their midst (Acts 5:1–11; 9:36–43; 20:7–10). As those early believers gathered they were keenly aware that the veil had been ripped in two and like Moses and Aaron they were entering the Holy of Holies. No intermediaries were needed. They were coming into the awful, glorious, gracious Presence of the living God. They gathered with anticipation, knowing that Christ was present among them and would teach them and touch them with His living power.

How do we cultivate this holy expectancy? It begins in us as we enter the Shekinah of the heart. While living out the demands of our day we are filled with inward worship and adoration. We work and play and eat and sleep, yet we are listening, ever listening, to our Teacher. The writings of Frank Laubach are filled with this sense of living under the shadow of the Almighty. "Of all today's miracles the greatest is this: to know that I find Thee best when I work listening. . . . Thank Thee, too, that the habit of constant conversation grows easier each day. I really do believe *all* thought can be conversations with Thee." [3]

Brother Lawrence knew the same reality. Because he experienced the presence of God in the kitchen he knew he would meet God in the Mass as well. He wrote, "I cannot imagine how religious persons can live satisfied without the practice of the Presence of God." [4] Those who have once tasted the Shekinah of God in daily experience can never again live satisfied without "practicing the Presence of God."

Catching the vision from Brother Lawrence and Frank Laubach, I dedicated one year recently to learning how to live with a perpetual openness to Jesus as my present Teacher. I determined to learn His vocabulary: is He addressing me through those singing birds or that sad face? I sought to allow Him to move through every action: these fingers as I wrote, this voice as I spoke. My desire was to punctuate each minute with inward whisperings of adoration, praise and thanksgiving. Often I failed for hours, even days at a time. But each time I came back and tried again. That year did many things for me, but the one I shall mention here is that it greatly heightened my sense of expectancy in public worship. After all, He had graciously spoken to me in dozens of little ways throughout the week; He will certainly speak to me here as well. In addition, I found it increasingly easier to distinguish His voice from the blare and circumstances of life.

When more than one or two come into public worship with a holy expectancy it can change the atmosphere of a room. People who enter harried and distracted are drawn quickly into a sense of the silent Presence. Hearts and minds are lifted upward. The air becomes charged with expectancy.

Here is a practical handle to put on this idea. Live throughout the week as an heir of the kingdom, listening for His voice, obeying His word. Since you have heard His voice throughout the week you know that you will hear His voice as you gather for public worship. Enter the service ten minutes early. Lift your heart in adoration to the King of glory. Contemplate His majesty, glory and tenderness as revealed in Jesus Christ. Picture the marvelous vision that Isaiah had of the Lord "high and lifted up" or the magnificent revelation that John had of Christ with eyes "like a flame of fire" and voice "like the sound of many waters" (Is. 6; Rev. 1). Invite the real Presence to be manifest. Fill the room with Light.

Next, lift into the Light of Christ the pastor or persons with particular responsibilities. Imagine the Shekinah of God's radiance surrounding him or her. Inwardly release them to speak the truth boldly in the power of the Lord.

By now people are beginning to enter. Glance around until your eyes catch some individual who needs your intercessory work. Perhaps their shoulders are drooped, or they seem a bit sad. Lift them into the glorious, refreshing Light of His Presence. Imagine the burden tumbling from their shoulders as it did from Pilgrim's in Bunyan's allegory. Hold them as a special intention throughout the service. If only a few in any given congregation would do this, it would deepen the worship experience of all.

Another vital feature of the early church community was their sense of being "gathered" together in worship. First, they were gathered in the sense that they actually met as a group, and second, as they met they were gathered into a unity of spirit that transcended their individualism.

In contrast to the religions of the East the Christian faith has strongly emphasized corporate worship. Even under highly dangerous circumstances the early community was urged not to forsake the assembling of themselves together (Heb. 10:25). The epistles speak frequently of the believing community as the "body of Christ." As human life is unthinkable without head, arms, and legs, so it was unthinkable for those Christians to live in isolation from one another. Martin Luther witnessed to the fact that "at home, in my own house, there is no warmth or vigor in me, but in the church when the multitude is gathered together, a fire is kindled in my heart and it breaks its way through."[5]

In addition, when the people of God meet together there often comes a sense of being "gathered" into one mind, becoming of one accord (Phil. 3:15). Thomas Kelly said: "A quickening Presence pervades us, breaking down some part of the special privacy and isolation of our individual lives and blending our spirits within a superindividual Life and Power. An objective, dynamic Presence enfolds us all, nourishes our souls, speaks glad, unutterable comfort with us, and quickens us in depths that had before been slumbering."[6] When we are truly gathered into worship, things occur that could never occur alone. There is the psychology of the group and yet it is much more, it is divine interpenetration. There is what the biblical writers called *koinonia,* deep inward fellowship in the power of the Spirit.

This experience far transcends *esprit de corps.* It is not in the least dependent upon homogeneous units or even knowing information about one another's lives. There comes a divine melting of our separateness. In the power of the one Spirit we become "wrapped in a sense of unity and of Presence such as quiets all words and enfolds [us] within an unspeakable calm and interknittedness within a vaster life."[7] Such fellowship-in-worship makes vicarious worship via the media tasteless and flat.

The Leader of Worship

Genuine worship has only one Leader, Jesus Christ. When I speak of Jesus as the Leader of worship I mean, first of all, that He is alive and present among His people. His voice can be heard in their hearts and His presence known. We not only read about Him in Scripture, we can know Him by revelation. He wants to teach us, guide us, rebuke us, comfort us.

Second, Christ is alive and present *in all His offices.* In worship we are prone to view Christ only in His priestly office, as Savior and Re-

deemer. But He is also among us as our Prophet. That is, He will
teach us about righteousness and give us the power to do what is right.
George Fox said, "Meet together in the Name of Jesus . . . he is
your Prophet, your Shepherd, your Bishop, your Priest, in the midst of
you, to open to you, and to sanctify you, and to feed you with Life,
and to quicken you with Life." [8]

Third, Christ is alive and present *in all His power.* He saves us not
only from the consequences of sin but from the domination of sin.
Whatever He teaches us He will give us the power to obey. If Jesus is
our Leader, miracles should be expected to occur in worship. Healings,
both inward and outward, will be the rule, not the exception. The
book of Acts will not just be something we read about but something
we are experiencing.

Fourth, Christ is the Leader of worship in the sense that He alone
decides what human instrumentalities are to be used, if any. Individuals preach, or prophesy, or sing, or pray as they are called forth by
their Leader. In this way there is no room for the elevation of private
reputations. Jesus alone is honored. As our living Head calls them
forth, any or all of the gifts of the Spirit can be freely exercised and
gladly received. Perhaps a word of knowedge is given in which the intent of the heart is revealed and we know that King Jesus is in charge.
Perhaps there is a prophecy or an exhortation that puts us on the edge
of our seat because we sense that the *Kol Yahweh* has been spoken.
Preaching or teaching that comes forth because the living Head has
called it forth breathes life into worship. Preaching that is without
divine unction will fall like a frost on the worship. Heart preaching
enflames the spirit of worship; head preaching smothers the glowing
embers. There is nothing more quickening than Spirit-inspired preaching, nothing more deadly than human-inspired preaching.

Avenues into Worship

One reason worship should be considered a spiritual Discipline is
because it is an ordered way of acting and living that sets us before
God so He can transform us. Although we are only responding to the
liberating touch of the Holy Spirit, there are divinely appointed avenues into this realm.

The first avenue into worship is to still all humanly initiated activity. The stilling of "creaturely activity," as the patriarchs of the inner life called it, is not something to be confined to worship services but is a life-style. It is to permeate the daily fabric of our lives. We are to live in a perpetual inward listening silence so that our words and actions have their source in God. If we are accustomed to carrying out the business of our lives in human strength and wisdom, we will do the same in gathered worship. If, however, we have cultivated the habit of allowing every conversation, every business transaction, to be divinely prompted, that same sensitivity will flow into public worship. François Fénelon said, "Happy the soul which by a sincere self-renunciation, holds itself ceaselessly in the hands of its Creator, ready to do everything which he wishes; which never stops saying to itself a hundred times a day, 'Lord, what wouldst thou that I should do?'"[9]

Does that sound impossible? The only reason we believe it to be far beyond us is that we don't understand Jesus as our present Teacher. When we have been under His tutelage for a time we see how it is possible for every motion of our lives to have its root in God. We wake up in the morning and lie in bed quietly praising and worshiping the Lord. We tell Him that we desire to live under His leadership and rule. Driving to work we ask our Teacher, "How are we doing?" Immediately our Mentor flashes before our mind that caustic remark we made to our spouse at breakfast, that shrug of disinterest we gave our children on the way out the door. We realize we have been living in the flesh. There is confession, restoration and a new humility.

We stop at the gas station and sense a divine urging to get acquainted with the attendant, to see him as a person rather than an automaton. We drive on, rejoicing in our new insight into Spirit-initiated activity. And so it goes throughout our day: a prompting here or a drawing there, sometimes a bolting ahead or a lagging behind our Guide. Like a child taking first steps we are learning through success and failure, confident that we have a present Teacher who through the Holy Spirit will guide us into all truth. In that way we come to understand what Paul meant when he instructed us to "walk not according to the flesh but according to the Spirit" (Rom. 8:4).

To still the activity of the flesh so that the activity of the Holy Spirit dominates the way we live will affect and inform public worship. Sometimes it will take the form of absolute silence. Certainly it is more fitting to come in reverential silence and awe before the Holy

One of Eternity than to rush into His Presence with hearts and minds askew and tongues full of words. The scriptural admonition is "The Lord is in his holy temple; let all the earth keep silence before him" (Hab. 2:20). The desert Father Ammonas wrote: "Behold, my beloved, I have shown you the power of silence, how thoroughly it heals and how fully pleasing it is to God. . . . It is by silence that the saints grew . . . it was because of silence that the power of God dwelt in them, because of silence that the mysteries of God were known to them."[10]

Praise brings us into worship. The psalms are the literature of worship and their most prominent feature is praise. "Praise the Lord!" is the shout that reverberates from one end of the Psalter to the other. Singing, shouting, dancing, rejoicing, adoring—all are the language of praise.

Scripture urges us to "offer the sacrifice of praise to God continually, that is, the fruit of our lips, giving thanks to his name (Heb. 13:15, KJV). The Old Covenant required the sacrifice of bulls and goats. The New Covenant requires the sacrifice of praise. Peter tells us that as Christ's new royal priesthood we are to offer "spiritual sacrifices," which means to "declare the wonderful deeds of him who called you out of darkness into his marvelous light" (1 Pet. 2:5, 9).

Peter and John left the Sanhedrin with bleeding backs and praising lips (Acts 5:41). Paul and Silas filled the Philippian jail with their songs of praise (Acts 16:25). In each case they were offering the sacrifice of praise.

The mightiest stirring of praise in the twentieth century has been the charismatic movement. Through it God has breathed new life and vitality into millions. In our day the church of Jesus Christ is coming into a greater awareness of how central praise is in bringing us into worship.

In praise we see how totally the emotions need to be brought into the act of worship. Worship that is solely cerebral is an aberration. Feelings are a legitimate part of the human personality and should be employed in worship. To make such a statement doesn't mean that our worship should do violence to our rational faculties, but it does mean that our rational faculties alone are inadequate. As Paul counseled, we are to pray with the spirit and pray with the mind, sing with the spirit and sing with the mind (1 Cor. 14:15). That is one reason for the spiritual gift of tongues. It helps us to move beyond mere rational worship into a more inward communion with the Father. Our outward mind may not know what is being said but our inward spirit understands. Spirit touches spirit.

Singing is meant to move us into praise. It provides a medium for the expression of emotion. Through music we express our joy, our thanksgiving. No less than forty-one psalms command us to "sing unto the Lord." If singing and praising can occur in a concentrated manner it serves to focus us. We become centered. Our fragmented minds and spirits flow into a unified whole. We become poised toward God.

God calls for worship that involves our whole being. The body, mind, spirit, and emotions should all be laid on the altar of worship. Often we have forgotten that worship should include the body as well as the mind and spirit.

The Bible describes worship in physical terms. The root meaning for the Hebrew word we translate *worship* is "to prostrate." The word *bless* literally means "to kneel." *Thanksgiving* refers to "an extension of the hand." Throughout Scripture we find a variety of physical postures in connection with worship: lying prostrate, standing, kneeling, lifting the hands, clapping the hands, lifting the head, bowing the head, dancing and wearing sackcloth and ashes. The point is that we are to offer God our bodies as well as all the rest of our being. Worship is appropriately physical.

We are to present our bodies to God in worship in a posture consistent with the inner spirit in worship. Standing, clapping, dancing, lifting the hands, lifting the head are postures consistent with the spirit of praise. To sit still, looking dour, is clearly inappropriate for praise. Kneeling, bowing the head, lying prostrate are postures consistent with the spirit of humility.

We are quick to object to this line of teaching. "People have different temperaments," we argue. "That may appeal to emotional types, but I'm naturally quiet and reserved. It isn't the kind of worship that would meet my need." What we must see is that the real question in worship is not "what will meet my need?" The real question is "what kind of worship does God call for?" It is clear that God calls for wholehearted worship. And it's as reasonable to expect wholehearted worship to be physical as to expect it to be cerebral.

Often our "reserved temperament" is little more than fear of what others will think of us, or perhaps unwillingness to humble ourselves before God and others. Of course people have different temperaments but that must never keep us from worshiping with our whole being.

We may of course do all the things I've described and never enter into worship, but they can provide avenues through which we are placed before God so that our inner spirit can be touched and freed.

The Consequences of Worship

If worship does not change us, it has not been worship. To stand before the Holy One of eternity is to change. Resentments cannot be held with the same tenacity when we enter His gracious light. As Jesus said, we will need to leave our gift at the altar and go set the matter straight (Mt. 5:23, 24). In worship an increased power steals its way into the heart sanctuary, an increased compassion grows in the soul. To worship is to change.

If worship does not propel us into greater obedience, it has not been worship. Just as worship begins in holy expectancy it ends in holy obedience. Holy obedience saves worship from becoming an opiate, an escape from the pressing needs of modern life. Worship enables us to hear the call to service clearly so that we respond, "Here I am! Send me" (Is. 6:8). Authentic worship will impel us to join in the Lamb's war against demonic powers everywhere, on the personal level, social level, institutional level. Jesus, the Lamb of God, is our commander-in-chief. We receive His orders for service and go in the mighty power of the Lord:

> . . . conquering and to conquer, not as the prince of this world
> . . . with whips and prisons, tortures and torments on the bod-
> ies of creatures, to kill and destroy men's lives . . . but with the
> word of truth . . . returning love for hatred, wrestling with God
> against the enmity, with prayers and tears night and day, with
> fasting, mourning and lamentation, in patience, in faithfulness,
> in truth, in love unfeigned, in long suffering, and in all the fruits
> of the spirit, that if by any means [we] may overcome evil with
> good. . . .[11]

Willard Sperry declared, "Worship is a deliberate and disciplined adventure in reality.[12] It is not for the timid or comfortable. It involves an opening of ourselves to the dangerous life of the Spirit. It makes all the religious paraphernalia of temples and priests and rites and ceremonies irrelevant. It involves a willingness to "let the word of Christ dwell in you richly, teach and admonish one another in all wisdom, and sing psalms and hymns and spiritual songs with thankfulness in your hearts to God" (Col. 3:16).

12. THE DISCIPLINE OF GUIDANCE

*Dwell in the life and love and power and wisdom of God,
in unity one with another and with God; and the peace and
wisdom of God fill your hearts, that nothing may rule in
you but the life, which stands in the Lord God
—George Fox*

In our day heaven and earth are on tiptoe waiting for the emerging of a
Spirit-led, Spirit-intoxicated, Spirit-empowered people. All of creation
watches expectantly for the springing up of a disciplined, freely gathered, martyr people who know in this life the life and power of the
kingdom of God. It has happened before. It can happen again.

Individuals can be found here and there whose hearts burn with
divine fire. But they are like flaming torches scattered in the night. As
yet there has been no gathering of a people of the Spirit.

Oh, there has been shouting, "Lo, here; lo, there," as Jesus warned
(Mt. 24:26). But such cries are only the temporary sparkle of human
fireworks, not the divine explosion of heavenly fire. Our century has
yet to see the breaking forth of the apostolic church of the Spirit.

Such a people will not emerge until there is among us a deeper,
more profound experience of an Emmanuel of the Spirit—God with
us, a knowledge that in the power of the Spirit Jesus has come to
guide His people Himself, an experience of His leading that is as definite and as immediate as the cloud by day and fire by night.

But the knowledge of the direct, active, immediate leading of the
Spirit will not be sufficient. Individual guidance must yield to corporate guidance. There must also come a knowledge of the direct, active, immediate leading of the Spirit *together*. I do not mean "corporate guidance" in an organizational sense but in an organic and
functional sense. Church councils and denominational decrees are simply not of this reality.

All the teaching on divine guidance in our century has been noticeably deficient on the corporate aspect. We have received excellent instruction on how God leads us through Scripture, and through circumstances, and through the promptings of the Spirit upon the individual heart. But we have heard little about how God leads through His people, the body of Christ. On that subject there is profound silence.

For this reason I have chosen to list guidance among the Corporate Disciplines and to stress its communal side. God does guide the individual richly and profoundly, but He also guides groups of people and can instruct the individual through the group experience.

Perhaps our preoccupation with private guidance is the product of our Western individualism. The people of God have not always been so.

God led the children of Israel out of bondage *as a people*. Everyone saw the cloud and fiery pillar. They were not a gathering of individuals who happened to be going in the same direction; they were a people under the theocratic rule of God. His brooding presence covered them with an amazing immediacy. The people, however, soon found God's unmediated presence too awful, too glorious, and begged, "Let not God speak to us, lest we die" (Ex. 20:19). So Moses became their mediator. Thus began the great ministry of the prophets whose function was to hear God's word and bring it to the people. It was a step away from the corporate leading of the Holy Spirit but there remained a sense of being a people together under the rule of God. But a day came when Israel rejected even the prophet in favor of a king. From that point on, the prophet was the outsider. He was a lonely voice crying in the wilderness, sometimes obeyed, sometimes killed, but always on the outside.

Patiently God prepared a people and in the fullness of time Jesus came. And with Him dawned a new day. Once again a people were gathered who would live under the immediate theocratic rule of the Spirit.

With quiet persistence Jesus showed them what it meant to live in response to the voice of the Father. He taught them that they, too, could hear the heaven-sent voice and, most clearly, when together. "If two of you agree on earth about anything they ask, it will be done for them by my Father in heaven. For where two or three are gathered in my name, there am I in the midst of them" (Mt. 18:19, 20).

In those words Jesus gave His disciples both assurance and authority. There was the assurance that when a people genuinely gathered in His name His will could be discerned. The superintending Spirit would utilize the checks and balances of the different believers to insure that when their hearts were in unity they were in rhythm with the heartbeat of the Father. Assured that they had heard the voice of the true Shepherd, they were able to pray and act with authority. His will plus their will plus unity equaled authority.

Although Jesus was an outsider to His own people, being crucified beyond the city gates, some people embraced His rulership. And they became a gathered people. "Now the company of those who believed were of one heart and soul, and no one said that any of the things which he possessed was his own, but they had everything in common. And with great power the apostles gave their testimony to the resurrection" (Acts 4:32, 33). They became a fiery band of witnesses declaring everywhere that Christ's voice could be heard and His will obeyed.

Perhaps the most astonishing feature of that incendiary fellowship was their sense of corporate guidance. It was beautifully illustrated in the calling forth of Paul and Barnabas to tramp the length and breadth of the Roman empire with the good news of the kingdom of God (Acts 13:1–3). Their call came when a number of people had been together over an extended period of time. It included the use of the Disciplines of prayer, fasting and worship. Having become a prepared people they received the call *together:* "Set apart for me Barnabas and Saul for the work to which I have called them" (Acts 13:2).

With all our modern methods of missionary recruitment we could profit by serious attention to that example of corporate guidance. We would be well advised to encourage groups of people who are willing to fast, pray and worship together until they have discerned the mind of the Lord and have heard His call.

Under corporate guidance the early church faced and resolved its most explosive issue (Acts 15). Some free-lance Christians had gone up to Antioch and had begun preaching the necessity of circumcision for all Christians. The issue was far from trivial. Paul saw at once that it was tantamount to the Jewish cultural captivity of the church.

Appointed elders and apostles gathered in the power of the Lord, not to jockey for position or to play one side against another, but to hear the mind of the Spirit. It was no small task. There was intense debate. Then in a beautiful example of how individual guidance impinges upon corporate guidance, Peter told about his experience with the Italian centurion Cornelius. As he spoke, the ever-brooding Spirit of God evidently did a wonderful work. When he finished, the entire assembly fell into silence (Acts 15:12). Finally, the gathered group struggled into what must be called a glorious heaven-sent unity to reject cultural religion and to hold to the everlasting gospel of Jesus Christ. They concluded, "It has seemed good to the Holy Spirit and to us . . ." (Acts 15:28). They had faced the toughest issue of their day and had discerned the voice from on high. There is the high-water mark in the book of Acts.

It was more than a victory regarding an issue; it was a victory of the method for resolving issues. As a people they had decided to live under the direct rulership of the Spirit. They had rejected both human totalitarianism and anarchy. They had even rejected democracy, that is, majority rule. They had dared to live on the basis of Spirit-rule; no 51 percent vote, no compromises, but Spirit-directed unity. And it worked.

No doubt those experiences in discerning the will of God in community contributed greatly to Paul's understanding of the church as the body of Christ. He saw that the gifts of the Spirit were given by the Spirit to the body in such a way that interdependence was insured. No one person possessed everything. Even the most mature needed the help of others. The most insignificant had something to contribute. No one could hear the whole counsel of God in isolation.

Sadly we must note that by the time John received his great apocalyptic vision the believing community was beginning to cool. By the time of Constantine the church was ready to accept another human king. The vision, however, did not die and there have been groups throughout the centuries gathered together under the rulership of the Spirit. Our century waits for such a gathering.

Some Models

The apostolic band did not leap from ground zero to the dizzy heights of Spirit-rulership in a single bound. Neither will we. For the most part they moved into that realm one step at a time, sometimes moving forward a bit, sometimes withdrawing. But by the time Pentecost had come they were a prepared people.

Having once understood the radical implications of being a people under the direct administration of the Holy Spirit, one of the most destructive things we can do is to say "Sounds wonderful; beginning tomorrow I'll live that way!" Such zealots only succeed in making life miserable for themselves and everyone around them. So, rather than sally off to conquer the world of the Spirit, most of us would be wise to be content with more modest steps for the present. One of the best ways we can learn is from models of people who have struggled corporately to hear the voice from on high.

One of the most delightful examples comes from "the poor little man of Assisi," St. Francis. Francis, it seems, was in "great agony of doubt" about whether he should devote himself only to prayer and meditation, which was a common practice in those days, or whether he should also engage in preaching missions. Wisely Francis sought out counsel. "As the holy humility that was in him did not allow him to trust in himself or in his own prayers, he humbly turned to others in order to know God's will in this matter."

He sent messages to two of his most trusted friends, Sister Clare and Brother Silvester, asking them to gather one of their "purer and more spiritual companions" with them and seek the will of God in the matter. Immediately they went to prayer and both Sister Clare and Brother Silvester returned with the same answer.

When the messenger returned, St. Francis first washed his feet and prepared him a meal. Then, kneeling down before the messenger, St. Francis asked him, "What does my Lord Jesus Christ order me to do?" The messenger replied that Christ had revealed that "He wants you to go about the world preaching, because God did not call you for yourself alone but also for the salvation of others." Receiving the message as the undisputed word of Christ, St. Francis jumped up saying, "So let's go—in the name of the Lord." [1] Whereupon he immediately embarked on a preaching mission. That direction gave the early Franciscan movement an unusual combination of mystical contemplation and evangelistic fervor.

In that experience Francis was doing more than seeking out the advice of wise counselors. He was seeking a method that would open the

gates of heaven to reveal the mind of Christ, and he took it as such—
to the great good of all to whom he ministered.

Another model for corporate guidance can be found in what some
have called "meetings for clearness." Such meetings are specifically
called to seek the mind of the Spirit for some individual's question.
Recently a gifted young man asked my counsel about his future. He
had graduated from college and was wrestling with whether or not to
go into the ministry. He had availed himself of all the vocational tests
and guidance courses offered and still was undecided. I honestly did
not know what was best for him and so suggested that he call a meeting for clearness. So he gathered a group of people who knew him
well, had spiritual maturity and were unafraid to be honest and candid
with him. There were no earth-shattering visions to give my friend,
but that night as they worshiped and shared they became a supporting
community. Over a period of time the gifts and calling of that young
man were confirmed and today he is in the pastoral ministry.

A concept closely akin to this has been pioneered by the Church of
the Saviour in Washington, D.C. When any member feels that God
has led him or her to establish a particular mission group or to venture
into a particular area of service they will "sound the call." That is
done at the conclusion of a worship service and the individual shares
the vision that he or she senses. Afterward all who would like to are
welcome to meet with the person to "test the call." Together they
probe the issue, praying, questioning, searching. Sometimes there is a
sense that the idea was the product of false enthusiasm and it is abandoned. At other times it is confirmed by the prayers and interaction of
the group. Perhaps others in the room are drawn into the call and make
it their own. Thus a "company of the committed" is formed.

Matters of the highest personal importance can be brought to the believing community for discernment. Recently two people came before
our community stating that they felt the leading of the Lord to be
married and desired the confirmation of a Spirit-directed body. Several
people who knew the couple well were asked to meet with them. This
is their report:

The special committee appointed to communicate with Mark
and Becky regarding their plans to marry is happy to return a
most positive report.

We met with Mark and Becky and had a most enjoyable evening of fellowship and prayer. We shared our concern for the sanctity of the family which is the heart of God's plan for human relationships. We were impressed with Mark and Becky's dependence upon the Lord's leading, their anticipation of potential problems, and their mature realization that successful marriage depends upon continuing commitment to each other and to the Lord.

We are happy to commend Mark and Becky's plans to the Newberg meeting. We feel their home will reflect the prayerful and loving influence of their childhood homes and the church community as they unite their love in that relationship ordained by God.

The committee feels a beneficial, special warmth for Mark and Becky which we anticipate will continue in a shepherding relationship. We recommend this precedent to other couples considering marriage.*

This is more than merely a rubber-stamping procedure. Not long ago two individuals in the fellowship decided to marry. Privately several counseled against the step though they seemed determined and had purchased a marriage license. Finally a couple whom the two trusted and respected encouraged them to bring the matter before the entire church and request a sense of corporate leading. They did so at the next scheduled meeting of the church (not on Sunday morning).

Tenderly and earnestly the couple shared their reasons for desiring marriage. An attitude of worship pervaded the group as questions were asked and responses made. At the close of the meeting the elders and other interested individuals were encouraged to continue to meet with the couple. The meeting was bathed with a deep sense of tenderness and prayer as the group sought to hear the mind of the Lord in the matter. After some time the entire group had a sense of unity and with an incredible spirit of compassion told the couple that they believed marriage at that time would be unwise.

For our group this was a new experience and it was extremely difficult to counsel them against their desires. Yet we felt clearly that we had rightly discerned the mind of Christ. Many of us waited for their

---

* Mark and Becky have given me permission to tell their story. The letter is on file in the Minutes of Newberg Friends Church, August 6, 1975.

response with fear and trembling. Questions loomed in our minds: "Did we come across like autocrats and lawgivers?" "Were we sufficiently sensitive to their feelings?"

Having received the discernment of the church body, the couple in a genuine act of spiritual maturity decided to postpone their marriage. Later they decided against marriage. Time has demonstrated the wisdom of their decision.*

That story underscores the importance of approaching such matters in the context of a loving community. Without a sense of support and caring, such matters can turn into soul-killing laws.

It is possible for business decisions to be made under a sense of the corporate leading of the Holy Spirit. Quakers have done so for years and have demonstrated the feasibility of such an approach. Business meetings should be viewed as worship services. Available facts can be presented and discussed, all with a view to listening to the voice of Christ. Facts are only one aspect of the decision-making process and in themselves are not conclusive. The Spirit can lead contrary to the available facts or in accord with them. He will implant a spirit of unity when the right path has been chosen and trouble us with restlessness when we have not heard Him correctly. Unity rather than majority rule is the principle of corporate guidance. Spirit-given unity goes beyond mere agreement. It is the perception that we have heard the *Kol Yahweh,* the voice of God.

A classic and dramatic illustration occurred in 1758. John Woolman and others had pricked the conscience of the Society of Friends over their involvement in the demonic institution of slavery. As Philadelphia Yearly Meeting gathered for its business meetings that year the slavery issue was a major agenda item. A great deal was at stake and the issue was hotly debated. John Woolman sat through the various sessions silent, with head bowed and tears in his eyes. Finally, after hours of agonizing prayer he rose and spoke.

My mind is led to consider the purity of the Divine Being and the justice of His judgment, and herein my soul is covered with awfulness. . . . Many slaves on this continent are oppressed

* Both individuals involved have given consent for the telling of their story. Neither has married as yet but both continue to "grow in the grace and knowledge of our Lord and Savior Jesus Christ" (2 Pet. 3:18).

and their cries have entered into the ears of the Most High. . . .
It is not a time for delay. Should we now be sensible of what he
requires of us, and through a respect to the private interests of
some persons, or through a regard to some friendships which do
not stand upon an immutable foundation, neglect to do our duty
in firmness and constancy . . . God may by terrible things in
righteousness answer us in this matter.[2]

The entire Yearly Meeting melted into a spirit of unity as a result of
this compassionate witness. They responded as one voice to remove
slavery from their midst. John Greenleaf Whittier stated that those sessions ''must ever be regarded as one of the most important religious
convocations in the history of the Christian Church.''[3]

That united decision is particularly impressive when we realize that
Quakers were the only body that asked slaveholders to reimburse their
slaves for their time in bondage.* It is also striking to realize that
under the prompting of the Spirit, Quakers had voluntarily done something that not one of the antislavery revolutionary leaders—George
Washington, Thomas Jefferson, Patrick Henry—was willing to do. So
influential had been that united decision of 1758 that by the time of the
signing of the Declaration of Independence Quakers had completely
freed themselves from the institution of slavery.

Many of the Christian communities springing up around the world
have discovered the reality and practicality of business decisions
through Spirit-rule. Such diverse groups as Reba Place Fellowship in
Illinois, Society of Brothers in New York, and the Mary Sisterhood in
Darmstadt, Germany, all operate on the basis of Spirit-directed unity.
Issues are approached with an assurance that the mind of the Spirit can
be known. They gather in Christ's name, believing that His will will
be fleshed out in their midst. They do not seek compromise but God-
given consensus.

I once attended a business session of some two hundred people in
which an issue had been earnestly debated. Though there was a sharp
difference of opinion, each of the members sincerely desired to hear
and obey the will of God. After a considerable period of time a united

* There are no accurate figures on the amount that was paid, though it was common to
pay the yearly wage at that time. In an appeal to the House of Commons to abolish slavery, one Mr. F. Buston said that it had cost North Carolina Friends 50,000 pounds to
release their slaves.

sense of direction began to emerge among everyone except for a few individuals. Finally one of these individual's stood and said, "I do not feel right about this course of action, but I hope that the rest of you will love me enough to labor with me until I have the same sense of God's leading as the rest of you or until God opens another way to us."

As an outside observer, I was touched by how tenderly the group responded to that appeal. All over the auditorium little groups began to gather to share, to listen, to pray. By the time they had broken through to a united decision I had received a far greater appreciation for the way in which Christians are to "maintain the unity of the Spirit in the bond of peace" (Eph. 4:3). Such expressions of the central function of corporate guidance are among the most healthy signs of spiritual vitality today.

The Spiritual Director

In the Middle Ages not even the greatest saints attempted the depths of the inward journey without the help of a spiritual director. Today the concept is hardly understood, let alone practiced, except in the Catholic monastic system. That is a tragedy for the idea of the spiritual director is highly applicable to the contemporary scene. It is a beautiful expression of divine guidance through the help of our brothers and sisters.

Spiritual directorship has an exemplary history. Many of the first spiritual directors were the desert Fathers and were held in high regard for their ability to "discern spirits." People would often travel for miles in the wilderness just to hear a brief word of advice, a "word of salvation," which summed up the will and judgment of God for them in their actual concrete situation. The *Apophthegmata* or "Sayings of the Fathers" is an eloquent testimony to the simplicity and depth of this spiritual guidance. Many of the Cistercian laybrothers in twelfth-century England were distinguished for their ability to read and guide souls.

What is the purpose of a spiritual director? The seventeenth-century Benedictine mystic, Dom Augustine Baker, wrote, "In a word, he is only God's usher, and must lead souls in God's way, and not his own."[4] His direction is simply and clearly to lead us to our real

Director. He is the means of God to open the path to the inward teaching of the Holy Spirit.

His function is purely and simply charismatic. He leads only by the force of his own personal holiness. He is not a superior or some ecclesiastically appointed authority. The relationship is of an advisor to a friend. Though the director has obviously advanced further into the inner depths, the two are together learning and growing in the realm of the Spirit.

All this talk of "soul" and "spirit" might lead us to think that spiritual direction deals only with a small corner or compartment of our lives. That is, we would go to a spiritual director to care for our spirit the way we might go to an ophthalmologist to care for our eyes. Such an approach is false. Spiritual direction is concerned with the whole person and the interrelationship of all of life. Thomas Merton told of a Russian spiritual director who was criticized for spending so much time earnestly advising an old peasant woman about the care of her turkeys. "Not at all," he replied, "her *whole life* is in those turkeys." [5] Spiritual direction takes up the concrete daily experiences of our lives and gives them sacramental significance. "So, whether you eat or drink, or whatever you do, do all to the glory of God" (1 Cor. 10:31).

Spiritual direction is first born out of natural, spontaneous human relationships. A hierarchical or even organizational system is not essential to its function and is often destructive to it. The ordinary kinds of caring and sharing that belong to the Christian community are the starting point for spiritual direction. Out of them will flow "kingdom authority" through mutual subordination and servanthood.

A spiritual director must be a person who has developed a comfortable acceptance of himself or herself. That is, a genuine maturity must pervade all of that person's life. Such persons are unmoved by the fluctuations of the times. They can absorb the selfishness and mediocrity and apathy around them and transform it. They are unjudging and unshakable. They must have compassion and commitment. Like Paul who thought of Timothy as his "beloved child," they must be prepared to take on certain parental responsibilities. Theirs must be a tough love that refuses to give approval to every whim. They should also know enough of the human psyche that they will not reinforce unconscious and infantile needs for authoritarianism.

A spiritual director must himself or herself be on the inward journey and be willing to share their own struggles and doubts. There needs to be a realization that together they are learning from Jesus, their present Teacher.

How is such a relationship arranged? As all other things in the kingdom of God, it is arranged by prayer. Bringing and resting our case with God we wait patiently for His way to be manifest. If He should invite us to speak to someone or make certain arrangements, we gladly obey. Such relationships can become formalized, as in some of the monastic orders, but they do not need to be. If we have the humility to believe that we can learn from our brothers and sisters and the understanding that some have gone further into the divine Center than others, we can see the necessity of spiritual direction. As Virgil Vogt of Reba Place Fellowship has said, "If you cannot listen to your brother, you cannot listen to the Holy Spirit." [6]

In reflecting on the value of this ministry for centuries of Christians, Thomas Merton said that the spiritual director was something of "a spiritual father who 'begot' the perfect life in the soul of his disciple by his instructions first of all, but also by his prayer, his sanctity and his example. He was . . . a kind of 'sacrament' of the Lord's presence in the ecclesiastical community." [7]

The Limits of Corporate Guidance

As we all know, dangers exist in corporate guidance as in individual guidance. Perhaps the most menacing danger is manipulation and control. If corporate guidance is not handled within the larger context of an all-pervasive grace, it degenerates into an effective way to straighten out deviant behavior. It becomes a kind of quasi-magic formula through which the group can impose its will upon the individual, a "papal system" through which all differing opinions can be brought into line.

Such manipulative perversion results in the stifling of fresh spiritual vitality. The prophet Isaiah tells us that the Messiah "will not break a bruised reed, or quench a smoldering wick" (Is. 42:3; Mt. 12:20). It is not the way of Jesus to crush the weakest person or to snuff out the smallest hope. Tenderness toward each individual situation must inform all our deliberations. On one occasion George Fox was debating, and roundly defeating, one Nathaniel Stephens. Overwhelmed, Stephens declared that "George Fox is come into the light of the sun, and now he thinks to put out my starlight." Fox wrote: "But I said, 'Nathaniel, give me thy hand'; then I told him I would not quench the least measure of God in any, much less put out his starlight." [8]

Another danger is that corporate guidance will become separate from biblical norms. Scripture must pervade and penetrate all of our thinking and acting. The one Spirit will never lead in opposition to the written Word which He inspired. There must always be the outward authority of Scripture as well as the inward authority of the Holy Spirit. In fact, Scripture itself is a form of corporate guidance. It is a way God speaks through the experience of the people of God. It is one aspect of "the communion of the saints."

Dallas Willard has said, "The aim of God in history is the creation of an all-inclusive community of loving persons, with Himself included in that community as its prime sustainer and most glorious inhabitant." [9] Such a community would live under the immediate and total rulership of the Holy Spirit. They would be a people blinded to all other loyalties by the splendor of God, a compassionate community embodying the law of love as seen in Jesus Christ. They would be an obedient army of the Lamb of God living under the Spiritual Disciplines, a community in the process of total transformation from the inside out, a people determined to live out the demands of the gospel in a secular world. They would be tenderly aggressive, meekly powerful, suffering and overcoming. Such a community, cast in a rare and apostolic mold, would constitute a new gathering of the people of God. May almighty God gather such a people in our day.

13. THE DISCIPLINE OF
CELEBRATION

The chief end and duty of man is to love God and to enjoy him forever.—The Westminister Cathechism

Celebration is at the heart of the way of Christ. He entered the world on a high note of jubilation: "I bring you good news of a great joy," cried the angel, "which shall come to all the people" (Lk. 2:10). He left the world bequeathing His joy to the disciples: "These things I have spoken to you that my joy may be in you, and that your joy may be full" (Jn. 15:11).

André Trocmé in *Jésus-Christ et la révolution non-violente* and later John Howard Yoder in *The Politics of Jesus* go to some length to demonstrate that Jesus began His public ministry by proclaiming the year of Jubilee (Lk. 4:18, 19). The social implications of such a concept are profound.* Equally penetrating is the realization that as a result we are called into a perpetual Jubilee of the Spirit. Such a radical, divinely enabled freedom from possessions and a restructuring of social arrangements cannot help but bring celebration. When the poor receive the good news, when the captives are released, when the blind receive their sight, when the oppressed are liberated, who could withhold the shout of Jubilee?

In the Old Testament all of the social stipulations of the year of Jubilee—canceling all debts, releasing slaves, no planting of crops, returning property to the original owner—were a celebration of the gracious provision of God. God could be trusted to provide what is

---

* Johannes Hoekendijk writes, "Jubilee is exodus spelled out in terms of social salvation. . . ." (*Union Seminary Quarterly Review,* "Mission—A Celebration of Freedom," Jan. 1966, p. 141)

163

needed. He had declared, "I will command my blessing upon you" (Lev. 25:21). Freedom from anxiety and care forms the basis for celebration. Because we know He cares for us we can cast all our care upon Him. God has turned our mourning into dancing.

The carefree spirit of joyous festivity is absent in contemporary society. Apathy, even melancholy, dominate the times. Harvey Cox says that modern man has been pressed "so hard toward useful work and rational calculation he has all but forgotten the joy of ecstatic celebration. . . ."[1]

Celebration Gives Strength to Life

Celebration brings joy into life, and joy makes us strong. Scripture tells us that the joy of the Lord is our strength (Neh. 8:10). We cannot continue long in anything without it. We may be able to begin piano lessons by dint of will, but we will not keep at them for long without joy. In fact, the only reason we can begin is because we know that joy is the end result. That is what sustains all novices: they know there is a sense of pleasure, enjoyment, joy in mastery.

Celebration is central to all the Spiritual Disciplines. Without a joyful spirit of festivity the Disciplines become dull, death-breathing tools in the hands of modern Pharisees. Every Discipline should be characterized by carefree gaiety and a sense of thanksgiving.

Joy is one of the fruits of the Spirit (Gal. 5:22). Often I am inclined to think that joy is the motor, the thing that keeps everything else going. Without joyous celebration to infuse the other Disciplines we will sooner or later abandon them. Joy produces energy. Joy makes us strong.

Ancient Israel was commanded to gather together three times a year to celebrate the goodness of God. Those were festival holidays in the highest sense. They were the experiences that gave strength and cohesion to the people of Israel.

The Path to Joy

In the spiritual life only one thing will produce genuine joy, and that is obedience. The old hymn tells us that there is no other way to be happy in Jesus but to "trust and obey." The hymn writer had received his inspiration from the Master himself, for Jesus tells us that there is no blessedness equal to the blessedness of obedience. On one occasion a woman in the crowd shouted out to Jesus, "Blessed is the womb that bore you, and the breasts that you sucked!" Jesus responded, "Blessed rather are those who hear the word of God and keep it!" (Lk. 11:27, 28). It is a more blessed thing to live in obedience than to have been the mother of the Messiah!

In 1870 Hannah Whitall Smith wrote what has come to be a classic on joyous Christianity, *The Christian's Secret of a Happy Life*. The title hardly hints at the depths of that perceptive book. It is no shallow "four easy steps to successful living." Studiously the writer defines the shape of a full and abundant life hid in God. Then she carefully reveals the difficulties to this way and finally charts the results of a life abandoned to God. What is the Christian's secret to a happy life? It could be best summed up by her chapter entitled "The Joy of Obedience." Joy comes through obedience to Christ and joy results from obedience to Christ. Without obedience joy is hollow and artificial.

To elicit genuine celebration obedience must work itself into the ordinary fabric of our daily lives. Without that our celebrating carries a hollow sound. For example, some people live in such a way that it is impossible to have any kind of happiness in their home, but then they go to church and sing songs and pray "in the Spirit" hoping that God will somehow give them an infusion of joy to make it through the day. They are looking for some kind of heavenly transfusion that will bypass the misery of their daily lives and give them joy. But God's desire is not to bypass the misery but to transform it.

We need to understand that God does at times give us an infusion of joy even in our bitterness and hardheartedness. But that is the abnormal situation. God's normal means of bringing His joy is by redeeming and sanctifying the ordinary junctures of human life. When the members of a family are filled with love and compassion and a spirit of service to one another, that family has a reason to celebrate.

There is something sad in anyone's running from church to church trying to get an injection of "the joy of the Lord." Joy is not found in singing a particular kind of music, or getting with the right kind of group, or even in exercising the charismatic gifts of the Spirit, good as all those may be. Joy is found in obedience. When the power that is in Jesus reaches into our work and play and redeems them, there will be joy where once there was mourning. To overlook that is to miss the meaning of the Incarnation.

That is why I have placed celebration at the end of this study. Joy is the end result of the Spiritual Disciplines' having functioned in our lives. God brings about the transformation of our lives through the Disciplines, and not until there is a transforming work within us do we know genuine joy. Many people try to come into joy far too soon. Often we try to pump up people with joy when in reality nothing has happened in their lives. God has not broken into the routine experiences of their daily existence. Celebration comes when the common ventures of life are redeemed.

It is important to avoid the kind of celebrations that really celebrate nothing. Worse yet is to pretend to celebrate when the spirit of celebration is not in us. Our children watch us bless the food and promptly proceed to gripe about it—blessings which are not blessings. One of the things that nearly destroys children is being forced to be grateful when they are not grateful. If we pretend an air of celebration our inward spirit is put in contradiction.

A popular teaching today instructs us to praise God for the various difficulties that come into our lives, asserting that there is great transforming power in thus praising God. In its best form such teaching is a way of encouraging us to look up the road a bit through the eye of faith and see what will be. It affirms in our hearts the joyful assurance that God takes all things and works them for the good of those who love Him. In its worst form this teaching denies the vileness of evil and baptizes the most horrible tragedies as the will of God. Scripture commands us to live in a spirit of thanksgiving in the midst of all situations; it does not command us to celebrate the presence of evil.

The Spirit of Carefree Celebration

The apostle Paul calls us to "rejoice in the Lord always; again I will say, Rejoice" (Phil. 4:4). But how are we to do that? "Have no anxiety about anything," or as the King James Version puts it, "Be careful for nothing." That is the negative side of rejoicing. The positive side is "in everything by prayer and supplication with thanksgiving let your requests be made known to God." And the result? "The peace of God, which passes all understanding, will keep your hearts and minds in Christ Jesus'' (Phil. 4:6, 7).

Paul instructed us on how we can always rejoice, and his first word of counsel was to be ''full of care'' for nothing. Jesus, of course, gave the same advice when He said, ''Do not be anxious about your life, what you shall eat or what you shall drink, nor about your body, what you shall put on'' (Mt. 6:25). In both instances the same word is used, which we translate ''anxious'' or ''careful.'' Christians are called to be free of care, but we find such a way foreign to us. We have been trained since we were two years old to be full of care. We shout to our children as they run to the school bus, ''Be careful,'' i.e., be full of care.

The spirit of celebration will not be in us until we have learned to be ''careful for nothing.'' And we will never have a carefree indifference to things until we totally trust God. This is why the Jubilee was such a crucial celebration in the Old Testament. No one would dare celebrate the Jubilee unless they had a deep trust in God's ability to provide for their needs.

When we trust God we are free to rely entirely upon Him to get what we need: ''By prayer and supplication with thanksgiving let your requests be made known to God.'' Prayer is the means by which we move the arm of God. Hence we can live in a spirit of carefree celebration.

Paul, however, did not end the matter there. He proceeded to tell us to set our minds on all the things in life that are true, honorable, just, pure, lovely and gracious. God has established a created order full of excellent and good things, and it follows naturally that if we think on those things we will be happy. That is God's appointed way to joy. If we think we will have joy only by praying and singing psalms we will be disillusioned. But if we fill our lives with simple good things and constantly thank God for them, we will know joy. And what about our problems? When we determine to dwell on the good and excellent things in life, our lives will be so full of those things that they will tend to swallow our problems.

The decision to set the mind on the higher things of life is an act of the will. That is why celebration is a Discipline. It is not something that falls on our head. It is the result of a consciously chosen way of thinking and living. As we choose that way, the healing and redemption in Christ will break into the inner recesses of our lives and relationships, and the inevitable result will be joy.

The Benefits of Celebration

Far and away the most important benefit of celebration is that it saves us from taking ourselves too seriously. That is a desperately needed grace for all those who are earnest about the Spiritual Disciplines. It is an occupational hazard of devout folk to become stuffy bores. That should not be. Of all people we should be the most free, alive, interesting. Celebration adds a note of gaiety, festivity, hilarity to our lives. After all, Jesus rejoiced so fully in life that He was accused of being a wine-bibber and a glutton. Many of us lead such sour lives that we couldn't possibly be accused of such things.

Now I am not recommending a periodic romp in sin, but I am suggesting that we do need deeper, more earthy experiences of exhilaration. It is healing and refreshing to cultivate a wide appreciation for life. Our spirit can become weary with straining after God, as our body can become weary with overwork. Celebration helps us to relax and enjoy the good things of the earth.

Celebration can be an effective antidote for the periodic sense of sadness that can constrict and oppress the heart. François Fénelon in his chapter titled "Helps in Sadness" counseled those who were bowed low with the burdens of life to encourage themselves "with good conversation, even by making merry."[2]

Celebration gives us perspective. We can laugh at ourselves. We come to see that the causes we champion are not nearly so monumental as we would like to believe.

In celebration the high and the mighty regain their balance and the weak and lowly receive new stature. Who can be high or low at the festival of God? Together the rich and the poor, the powerful and the powerless all celebrate the glory and wonder of God. There is no leveler of caste systems like festivity.

Thus freed of an inflated view of our own importance we are also freed of a judgmental spirit. Others do not look so awful, so unspiritual. Common joys can be shared without subjecting them to sanctimonious value judgments.

Finally, an interesting characteristic of celebration is that it tends toward more celebration. Joy begets joy. Laughter begets laughter. It is one of those few things in life that by giving we multiply. Kierkegaard said that "humor is always a concealed pair." [3]

The Practice of Celebration

If celebration is primarily a corporate Discipline, and if it brings such benefit to the people of God, how is it practiced? The question is a good one, for modern men and women have become so mechanized that we have snuffed out nearly all experiences of spontaneous joy. Our experiences of celebration are artificial, plastic.

Because of the goodness of God the heart breaks forth into psalms and hymns and spiritual songs. Worship, praise, adoration, dancing, laughing, flow from the inner chambers. The psalmist declared, "The earth is the Lord's and the fullness thereof" (Ps. 24:1). In Psalm 150 we see the celebration of the people of God with trumpet and lute and harp, with timbrel and dance, with strings and pipe and loud clashing cymbals.

What do little children do when they celebrate? They make noise, lots of noise. There is not a thing wrong with noise at the appropriate time, just as there is nothing wrong with silence when it is appropriate. Children dance when they celebrate. David went leaping and dancing before the Lord with all his might (2 Sam. 6:14, 16). When the children of Israel had been snatched from the clutches of Pharaoh by the might power of God, Miriam the prophetess led the people in a great celebration dance (Ex. 15:20). The folk dance has always been a carrier of cultural values and has been used repeatedly in genuine celebration. Of course dancing can have wrong and evil manifestations, but that is another matter entirely.

Dancing and noise-making are not required forms of celebration. They are examples only, to impress upon us that the earth indeed is the Lord's and the fullness thereof. Like Peter we need to learn that nothing is unclean that comes from the gracious hand of God (Acts 10). We are free to celebrate the goodness of God with all our viscera!

We can do some specific things to cultivate the art of celebration. One is to accent the creative gifts of fantasy and imagination. Harvey Cox has observed that "man's celebrative and imaginative faculties have atrophied."[4] In another place he writes, "There was a time when visionaries were canonized, and mystics were admired. Now they are studied, smiled at, perhaps even committed. All in all, fantasy is viewed with distrust in our time."[5]

We of the New Age can risk going against the tide. Let us with abandon relish the fantasy games of children. Let's see visions and dream dreams. Let's play, sing, laugh. The imagination can release a flood of creative ideas, and exercising our imagination can be lots of fun. Only those who are insecure about their own maturity will fear such a delightful form of celebration.

Another thing we can do is to make family events into times of celebration and thanksgiving. This is particularly true of the various rites of passage in our culture like birthdays and graduations. But it should also be true of lesser but equally important events. Why allow Halloween to be a pagan holiday in commemoration of the powers of darkness? Fill the house or church with light; sing and celebrate the victory of Christ over darkness. Let the children (and adults) dress up as biblical characters or as some of the saints through the centuries. In addition, form regular rituals of celebration that are not connected with historic events but that belong to your family alone. Spend more time around the piano as a family and sing out! Learn the folk dances of various cultures and enjoy them together.

A third thing we can do is to take advantage of the festivals of our culture and really celebrate. Christmas may be a lost cause but Easter certainly is not. Forget the spring style show and celebrate the power of the resurrection. Make family Easter plays. Revive the May Day celebrations. Go pick flowers and deliver them to your neighbors and friends. Rejoice in the beauty of color and variety.

In the Middle Ages there was a holiday known as the Feast of Fools.[6] It was a time when all "sacred cows" of the day could be safely laughed at and mocked. Minor clerics mimicked and ridiculed their superiors. Political leaders were lampooned. We can do without the excessive debauchery that often accompanied those festivities, but we do need an occasion to laugh at ourselves. Instead of chafing under and fighting against the social customs of our day we might do well to find ways to laugh at them.

We are not limited to established festivals; we can develop our own. Recently our church fellowship had a celebration night in appreciation of the pastors. Each family designed a homemade card. Various groups prepared skits, plays, readings, jokes. As one of those pastors, I can say that it was a hilarious night.

Celebration gives us the strength to live in all the other Disciplines. The other Disciplines faithfully pursued bring us deliverance from those things that have made our lives miserable for years, which in turn evokes increased celebration. Thus is formed an unbroken circle of life and power.

Finis

We have come to the end of this study but only to the beginning of our journey. We have seen how *meditation* heightens our spiritual sensitivity, which in turn leads us into *prayer*. Very soon we discover that prayer involves *fasting* as an accompanying means. Informed by these three Disciplines we can effectively move into *study* which gives us discernment about ourselves and the world in which we live.

Through *simplicity* we live with others in integrity. *Solitude* allows us to be genuinely present to people when we are with them. Through *submission* we live with others without manipulation, and through *service* we are a blessing to them.

Confession frees us from ourselves and releases us to *worship*. Worship opens the door to *guidance*. All the Disciplines freely exercised bring forth the doxology of *celebration*.

The classical Disciplines of the spiritual life beckon us to the Himalayas of the Spirit. Now we stand at timberline awed by the snowy peaks before us. We step out in confidence with our Guide who has blazed the trail and conquered the highest summit.

At times we may become discouraged in our journey. The peaks, where we would like to be, look so distant. We are painfully aware of our seemingly endless wanderings in the foothills. But when we look back we see that progress has been made and in that we rejoice.

The apostle Paul knew that he had many heights yet to conquer. Rather than being discouraged, however, he was challenged to "press on toward the goal for the prize of the upward call of God in Christ Jesus" (Phil. 3:14). The same challenge is ours today.

NOTES

===

Chapter 1

1. John Woolman, *The Journal of John Woolman* (Secaucus, New Jersey: The Citadel Press, 1972), p. 118.
2. Thomas Merton, *Contemplative Prayer* (Garden City, New York: Doubleday & Co., Inc., 1969), p. 37.
3. Heini Arnold, *Freedom from Sinful Thoughts: Christ Alone Breaks the Curse* (Rifton, New York: Plough Publishing House, 1973), p. 94.
4. *Ibid.*, p. 64.
5. *Ibid.*, p. 82.
6. Frank S. Mead, ed., *Encyclopedia of Religious Quotations* (London: Peter Davis Ltd., 1965), p. 400.

Chapter 2

1. Morton T. Kelsey, *The Other Side of Silence: A Guide to Christian Meditation* (New York: Paulist Press, 1976), p. 83.
2. R. D. Laing, *The Politics of Experience* (New York: Random House, Patheon Books, 1967), p. 101.
3. Thomas Merton, *Spiritual Direction and Meditation* (Minnesota: The Liturgical Press, 1960), p. 59.
4. Morton Kelsey in *The Other Side of Silence* makes an excellent analysis of Eastern and Christian meditation. See especially pp. 1, 57, 98 and 121.
5. Merton, *op. cit.*, p. 6.

6. Peter-Thomas Rohrbach, *Conversation with Christ* (Chicago: Fides Publishers, Inc., 1956), p. 31.

7. Elizabeth O'Connor, *Search for Silence* (Waco, Texas: Word Books, 1971), p. 117.

8. Thomas Merton, *Contemplative Prayer* (Garden City, New York: Doubleday & Co., 1971), p. 39.

9. O'Connor, *op. cit.,* p. 116.

10. Kelsey, *op. cit.,* p. 62.

11. Merton, *Spiritual Direction and Meditation,* p. 47.

12. Merton, *Contemplative Prayer,* p. 29.

13. A. W. Tozer, *The Knowledge of the Holy* (New York: Harper & Brothers, 1961), p. 20.

14. O'Connor, *op. cit.,* p. 95.

15. Merton, *Spiritual Direction and Meditation,* p.98.

16. Merton, *Contemplative Prayer,* p. 59.

17. Merton, *Spiritual Direction and Meditation,* p. 75.

18. St. Francis de Sales, *Introduction to the Devout Life,* trans. John K. Ryan (New York: Doubleday & Co., 1955), p. 84.

19. Kelsey, *op. cit.,* p. 167.

20. *Ibid.,* p. 207.

21. Agnes Sanford, *The Healing Gifts of the Spirit* (New York: J. B. Lippincott Co., 1966), p. 22.

22. Evelyn Underhill, *Practical Mysticism* (New York: E. P. Dutton & Co., Inc., 1943), p. 90.

23. de Sales, *op. cit.,* p. 83.

24. Dietrich Bonhoeffer, *The Way to Freedom* (New York: Harper & Row, 1966), p. 59.

25. Merton, *Spiritual Direction and Meditation,* pp. 88–89.

Chapter 3

1. E. M. Bounds, *Power Through Prayer* (Chicago: Moody Press, n.d.), p. 23.

2. *Ibid.,* p. 38.

3. *Ibid.,* pp. 38, 77.

4. *Ibid.,* pp. 41, 54.

5. *Ibid.,* p. 13.

6. Merton, *Contemplative Prayer,* p. 11.

7. Søren Kierkegaard, *Christian Discourses,* trans. Walter Lowie (Oxford University Press, 1940), p. 324.

8. Meister Eckhart, *Meister Eckhart,* trans. C. de B. Evans, Vol. I (London: John M. Watkins, 1956), p. 59.

9. Lynn J. Radcliffe, *Making Prayer Real* (New York: Abington-Cokesbury Press, 1952), p. 214.

10. Frank C. Laubach, *Prayer the Mightiest Force in the World* (New York: Fleming H. Revell Co., 1946), p. 31.

11. Frank C. Laubach, *Learning the Vocabulary of God* (Nashville: The Upper Room Publishing Co., 1956), p. 33.

12. Bounds, *op. cit.,* p. 83.

13. Thomas R. Kelly, *A Testament of Devotion* (New York: Harper & Brothers Publishers, 1941), p. 124.

14. *Ibid.,* p. 35.

15. Bounds, *op. cit.,* p. 35.

Chapter 4

1. John Wesley, *The Journal of the Reverend John Wesley* (London: The Epworth Press, 1938), p. 147.

2. David R. Smith, *Fasting: A Neglected Discipline* (Fort Washington, Pennsylvania: Christian Literature Crusade, 1969), p. 6.

3. Arthur Wallis, *God's Chosen Fast* (Fort Washington, Pennsylvania: Christian Literature Crusade, 1971), p. 25.

4. Dietrich Bonhoeffer, *The Cost of Discipleship* (New York: The Macmillan Co., 1959), p. 47.

5. Bounds, *op. cit.,* p. 25.

6. John Wesley, *Sermons on Several Occasions* (London: Epworth Press, 1971), p. 301.

7. Smith, *op. cit.,* p. 39.

8. Kelly, *op. cit.,* p. 35.

9. Wallis, *op. cit.,* p. 66.

10. O'Connor, *op. cit.,* pp. 103, 104.

11. Wesley, *Sermons on Several Occasions,* p. 297.

Chapter 5

1. Martin Buber, *Tales of the Hasidim: Early Masters* (New York: Schocken Books, Inc., 1948), p. 111.

2. André Gide, *If It Dies,* trans. Dorothy Bussey (New York: Random House, 1935), p. 83.

3. Evelyn Underhill, *Practical Mysticism* (New York: World Publishing Co., Meridian Books, 1955), pp. 93–94.

4. Fyodor Dostoevski, *The Brothers Karamazov* (Chicago: Encyclopedia Britannica, Great Books, 1952), p. 167.

5. Charles Noel Douglas, Ed., *Forty Thousand Quotations* (Garden City, New York: Halcyon House, 1940), p. 1680.

Chapter 6

1. Richard E. Byrd, *Alone* (G. P. Putnam's Sons, Inc., 1938), p. 19.
2. Arthur G. Gish, *Beyond the Rat Race* (New Canaan, Connecticut: Keats Publishing, Inc., 1973), p. 21.
3. *Ibid.*, p. 20.
4. Kierkegaard, *op. cit.*, p. 322.
5. *Ibid.*, p. 27.
6. Wesley, *Journal*, Nov. 1767.
7. Ronald J. Sider, *Rich Christians in an Age of Hunger* (Downers Grove, Illinois: InterVarsity Press, 1977), p. 18.
8. Kierkegaard, *op. cit.*, p. 344.
9. Woolman, *Journal*, pp. 144–145.
10. *Ibid.*, p. 168.
11. George Fox, *Works* (Philadelphia, 1831, Vol. 8), p. 126 Epistle #131.

Chapter 7

1. O'Connor, *op. cit.*, p. 132.
2. Dietrich Bonhoeffer, *Life Together* (New York: Harper & Row, 1952), pp. 77, 78.
3. Catherine de Hueck Doherty, *Poustinia: Christian Spirituality of the East for Western Man* (Notre Dame: Ave Maria Press, 1974), p. 23.
4. Thomas à Kempis, *The Imitation of Christ* (New York: Pyramid Publications, Inc., 1967), p. 18.
5. Woolman, *Journal*, p. 11.
6. Bonhoeffer, *op. cit.*, p. 79.
7. Doherty, *op. cit.*, p. 212.
8. St. John of the Cross, *The Collected Works of St. John of the Cross*, trans. Kieran Kavanaugh and Otilio Rodriguez (Garden City, New York: Doubleday & Co., Inc., 1964), p. 296.
9. *Ibid.*, p. 363.
10. *Ibid.*, p. 295.
11. *Ibid.*, p. 364.
12. *Ibid.*, p. 365.
13. Bonhoeffer, *op. cit.*, p. 80.
14. Thomas Merton, *The Sign of Jonas* (New York: Harcourt, Brace and Co., 1953), p. 261.
15. Doherty, *op. cit.*, p. 216.

Chapter 8

1. Thomas à Kempis, *The Imitation of Christ* in an anthology entitled *The Consolation of Philosophy* (New York: Random House Publishers, 1943), p. 139.
2. *Hymns for Worship* (Nappanee, Indiana: Evangel Press, 1963), p. 248.
3. John Howard Yoder, *The Politics of Jesus* (Grand Rapids: William B. Eerdmans Publishing Co., 1972), pp. 181–182. (I am indebted to Yoder for several of the ideas that follow.)
4. *Ibid.,* p. 181.
5. *Ibid.,* p. 186.
6. Kempis, *op. cit.,* p. 172.

Chapter 9

1. Kelly, *A Testament of Devotion* p. 124.
2. St. Francis of Assisi, *Selections from the Writings of St. Francis of Assisi* (Nashville: The Upper Room Press, 1952), p. 25.
3. John Milton, *The Complete Works of John Milton* (New York: Crown Publishers, 1936), p. 614.
4. C. H. Dodd as quoted in William Barclay, *The Letters of John and Jude* (Philadelphia: The Westminster Press, 1960), pp. 68, 69.
5. William Law, *A Serious Call to a Devout and Holy Life* (Nashville: The Upper Room Press, 1952), p. 26.
6. Kempis, p. 211.
7. Brother Ugolino di Monte Santa Maria, *The Little Flowers of St. Francis*(Garden City, New York: Doubleday & Co., 1958), pp. 58–60.
8. Dietrich Bonhoeffer, *The Cost of Discipleship* (New York: The Macmillan Co., 1963), p. 188.
9. Jeremy Taylor, *The Rule and Exercises of Holy Living* in *Fellowship of the Saints: An Anthology of Christian Devotional Literature* (New York: Abingdon-Cokesbury Press, 1957), p. 353.
10. Bonhoeffer, *Life Together,* p. 99.
11. François Fénelon, *Christian Perfection* (Minneapolis: Bethany Fellowship Inc., 1975), p. 34.
12. *Ibid.,* p. 36.
13. Bernard of Clairvaux, *St. Bernard on the Song of Songs* (London: A. R. Mowbray & Co., 1952), p. 70.
14. Bonhoeffer, *Life Together,* p. 97.
15. *Ibid.,* p. 98.

Chapter 10

1. Bonhoeffer, *Life Together,* p. 112.
2. *Ibid.,* p. 118.
3. Agnes Sanford, *op. cit.,* p. 110.
4. Bonhoeffer, *Life Together,* p. 116.
5. St. Alphonsus Liguori, "A Good Confession," found in an anthology entitled *To Any Christian* (London: Burns & Oates, 1964), p. 192.
6. Douglas Steere, *On Beginning from Within* (New York: Harper & Brothers, 1943), p. 80.
7. Liguori, *op. cit.,* p. 193.
8. Geoffrey Chaucer, *The Canterbury Tales* (Baltimore: Penguin Books, 1959), p. 23.
9. Bounds, *op. cit.,* p. 77.
10. Liguori, *op. cit.,* p. 195.
11. Bonhoeffer, *Life Together,* p. 118. (The phrase "living under the cross" is Bonhoeffer's.)
12. Sanford, *op. cit.,* p. 117.

Chapter 11

1. Tozer, *op. cit.,* p. 11.
2. *Ibid.,* p. 21.
3. Frank C. Laubach, *Learning the Vocabulary of God,* pp. 22–23.
4. Brother Lawrence, *The Practice of the Presence of God* (Nashville: The Upper Room Publishing Co., 1950), p. 32.
5. Douglas Steere, *Prayer and Worship* (New York: The Edward W. Hazen Foundation, Inc., 1942), p. 36.
6. Kelly, *The Eternal Promise,* p. 72.
7. *Ibid.,* p. 74.
8. George Fox, Epistle #288 (1672), quoted in *Quaker Religious Thought* (Vol. 15, No. 2 Winter 1973–74), p. 23.
9. Fénelon, *op. cit.,* p. 4.
10. Thomas Merton, *Contemplative Prayer,* p. 42.
11. James Nayler, *A Collection of Syndry Books, Epistles, and Papers, Written by James Nayler,* etc. (Printed in London, 1716), p. 378.
12. Willard Sperry, "Reality in Worship" taken from *The Fellowship of Saints: An Anthology of Christian Devotional Literature,* Thomas S. Kepler, Ed. (New York: Abingdon-Cokesbury Press, 1963), p. 685.

Chapter 12

1. Brother Ugolino, *op. cit.,* pp. 74–78.
2. Rufus M. Jones, *The Quakers in the American Colonies* (New York: W. W. Norton and Co., 1921), p. 517.
3. John G. Whittier, ed., *The Journal of John Woolman* (London: Headley Brothers, 1900), p. 13.
4. Thomas Merton, *Spiritual Direction and Meditation,* p. 12.
5. *Ibid.,* p. 8.
6. Dave and Neta Jackson, *Living Together in a World Falling Apart* (Carol Stream, Illinois: Creation House, 1974), p. 101.
7. Merton, *Spiritual Direction and Meditation,* p. 9.
8. George Fox, *The Journal of George Fox* (London: Headley Brothers Ltd., 1975), p. 184.
9. Dallas Willard, *Studies in the Book of Apostolic Acts: Journey into the Spiritual Unknown* (unpublished study guide available only from the author).

Chapter 13

1. Harvey Cox, *The Feast of Fools* (Cambridge: Harvard University Press, 1969), p. 12.
2. Fénelon, *op. cit.,* p. 102.
3. D. Elton Trueblood, *The Humor of Christ* (New York: Harper & Row, 1964), p. 33.
4. Cox, *op. cit.,* p. 11.
5. *Ibid.,* p. 10.
6. *Ibid.,* p. 3.